CAREER DIARY
OF A
COMPOSER

Thirty days behind the scenes with a professional.

GARDNER'S GUIDE® SERIES

PATRICK SMITH

GGC

GARTH GARDNER COMPANY

GGC publishing

Washington DC, USA · London, UK

Cover Designer: Nic Banks
Layout Designer: Rachelle Painchaud-Nash
Editor: Chris Edwards
Publisher: Garth Gardner, Ph.D.

Editorial inquiries concerning this book should be mailed to: The Editor, Garth Gardner Company, 5107 13th Street N.W., Washington DC 20011 or emailed to: info@ggcinc.com. http://www.gogardner.com

Copyright © 2006, GGC, Inc. All rights reserved.

No part of this book may be reproduced, stored in a retrieval system, or transmitted in any form or by any other means—electronic, mechanical, photocopying, recording, or otherwise —except for citations of data for scholarly or reference purposes, with full acknowledgment of title, edition, and publisher, and written notification to GGC/Publishing prior to such use.

GGC/Publishing is a department of Garth Gardner Company, Inc. and Gardner's Guide is a registered trademark of Garth Gardner Company, Inc.

ISBN: 1-58965-024-7

Library of Congress Cataloging-in-Publication Data

Smith, Patrick, 1949-
　Career diary of a composer / by Patrick Smith.
　p. cm. -- (Gardner's guide series)
　1. Computer sound processing. 2. Computer music--History and criticism. 3. Music trade--Vocational guidance.
4. Composition (Music)　　I. Title. II. Series.

MT723.S53 2006
780.23--dc22

　　　　　　　　　　　　　　　　　　　　　　2006000786

Printed in Canada

TABLE OF CONTENTS

- 5 Introduction: Author's Biography
- 15 Day 1
- 21 Day 2
- 25 Day 3
- 29 Day 4
- 33 Day 5
- 37 Day 6
- 39 Day 7
- 41 Day 8
- 45 Day 9
- 49 Day 10
- 53 Day 11
- 59 Day 12
- 63 Day 13
- 67 Day 14
- 71 Day 15
- 75 Day 16
- 79 Day 17
- 81 Day 18
- 85 Day 19
- 91 Day 20
- 95 Day 21
- 99 Day 22
- 103 Day 23
- 109 Day 24
- 113 Day 25
- 119 Day 26
- 123 Day 27
- 129 Day 28
- 137 Day 29
- 143 Day 30

BIOGRAPHY

My hometown is a little burg in rural Indiana, surrounded on all sides by cornfields stretching from horizon to horizon. There are signs at the city limits along all the (four) main roads into town that read: "Welcome to North Manchester, Indiana, home of 5,477 contented citizens, and a few old soreheads." It was home to Manchester College, a small liberal-arts institution where everyone majored in some academic field, and minored in basketball.

I grew up in probably the most middle of middle-America, one of the gazillion baby-boomers who burst upon the world in the middle of the twentieth century, the pride and joys of our postwar parents who had absolutely no bloody idea what they were in for. It was probably better that way, because otherwise they might have drowned us.

Rural Indiana, quite frankly, has never been known for producing many great and famous artists, writers and musicians, although Indiana University can rightly boast one of the finest music schools in the country. I, however, did not go there.

I began playing piano pretty much as soon as I could

reach one. We had an old upright piano in the basement that I was fond of abusing. I used to pound out dramatic-sounding stuff, and would sometimes stick things in between the strings to make them buzz or klunk in funny ways. It wasn't until some years later when I first heard about fellows like John Cage and others experimenting with "prepared piano" and said: "Hey, I used to do that all the time!" I wonder if John Cage's parents used to yell at him about it, too.

We always had some kind of piano around the house. My mother and her brother had performed as a duo act when they were young and had appeared on radio occasionally. So Mom would still play sometimes, although she eventually weaned herself from it totally.

We also kept a good number of records around the house, mostly big band jazz and some light classics, all of which I loved and played until they wore out. At the time my parents owned what they called a "sundries" store, which was something like a pharmacy, but without a pharmacist. They sold every kind of small item imaginable, from over-the-counter drugs to plastic vomit, and they also sold pop records. My mother would watch "American Bandstand" religiously to try to find out what the next big sellers were going to be.

I took classical piano lessons when I was seven or eight from what had to be the oldest living woman on the planet (of course at that age, anyone much over

30 looked pretty long in the tooth to me), and I was incorrigible. I wanted to play jazz, compose, and improvise, and she wanted me to play scales and learn to read music.

When I was 12, my father got an attractive job offer from a fellow he had known for some years, and taking it required us to relocate. We were moving up off the farm and out of the woods, to the bright lights and bustle of the "big city," Dayton, Ohio. Actually, to another 5000-or-so populated town just to the north, but as far as I was concerned, it was close enough to almost be Hollywood!

In school, I played clarinet in the marching and concert bands, and managed to become principle clarinet on the strength of my ability to disguise the fact that I couldn't read music worth a crap with a good sense of tone and style, and the musical ear and memory to be able to quickly pick up on what was being played by whoever sat next to me.

But keyboards remained my real passion, and by the time I was 15, I had quit the school bands and started a little rock-and-roll group with some friends, with myself playing a beat-up electric organ upon which I often had to perform emergency surgery in mid-show. Over time, one band led to another, and I eventually got with a band that stayed together for the next ten years, performing all over the (mostly south-eastern) United

States, doing a lot of writing and studio recording, and ultimately going broke like everybody else. But it was the studio experience that made the whole thing worthwhile in the longer term.

I eventually landed in the Washington, DC area after a separation with my wife of the time, in an ultimately unsuccessful attempt to reconcile. Upon our breakup, I worked at several music stores and record shops where my peculiar way of looking at things seemed to have some value. I played with local and road bands of various types, and did freelance studio work in DC, Nashville, Florida, New York, and a number of other places.

While floating around in this nether-world of on-again off-again employment, I happened to get invited to a party by a cute young lady to whom I had sold a stereo, so I went to this little gathering at a house near American University where I knew no one. Whenever I find myself in such situations, I often find it a good ice-breaker to locate the nearest piano and start playing, and sure enough, there was a nice little baby grand in the living room. I sat down and began fooling around, and soon a couple other musicians brought their instruments around, and a little impromptu jam session ensued.

While I was playing, a fellow came up to the piano and handed me a business card. He was the chief engineer and producer at a recording studio in Northwest DC, and since I was looking for work, I gave him a call a couple days later.

The studio held the rather unimpressive name of "Sounds Reasonable," and the guy from the party was Jim Harmon, who gave me a tour of the place and we talked about what I did and what they did, and we made a deal to record a few tunes of mine with some creative financing options. Shortly thereafter, I disappeared back on the road with yet another rock-and-roll band for about a year.

While I was AWOL, the owner of Sounds Reasonable disappeared as well, along with his secretary. Harmon found himself holding the bag for the business and it's bills, and it wasn't long before the SBA foreclosed on the loans they made to the company and seized the remaining assets. With nowhere to go but up, Harmon managed to cobble together a group of investors, and bought the studio's assets back from the SBA at fire-sale prices. The new company, called: "Soundwave," then set about to make the transition from a rock-and-roll studio to a film and video post production house.

When I returned from the road, being the ethical fellow that I am, I went to the studio to pay off (part of) what I owed them, and Harmon told me the tale of the runaway owner and the buy-back etc., and that my debt to Sounds Reasonable no longer existed. That sounded very reasonable to me.

It was there that I got my first film composition assignment, a recruitment film for the National Guard. From that point on, more scoring jobs began to trickle in, one year there would be three, the next, eight, the year after that, 15, and so on, almost all of them filtering through Soundwave. Eventually, Harmon decided it might be more cost-effective to just put me on the staff rather than to be cutting a special check every few weeks.

We then created a music-composition subsidiary called: Waveworks Music, and I moved into a small office/studio with a sliding glass door though which clients could watch me in the very act of creation. It's a frightening thought.

I have now been with the company for over 15 years, and in that time, I have composed music for television, radio, and internet-related purposes, for such clients as the Smithsonian, the National Gallery of Art, NASA, Fox Television, Discovery Channel, many, if not most, of the membership of Congress, and the last five U.S. presidents. I have a compiled music library of over 1300 compositions, but there are probably upwards of a thousand more that I am still in the process of cataloging.

It's not Hollywood, nor is it New York. Its seems the

bigger film and television producers usually only come to our town to do some location shooting, and maybe grab a little b-roll of the Capitol and the White House, then they beat hell back to their respective coasts as fast as jet airplane technology can carry them, climb into their hot tubs with their frozen margaritas in hand and sigh, "Thank GOD we're outta there"!

But composing music for the kind of stuff that is produced here presents a lot of unique challenges and opportunities you do not find anywhere else. The political orientation of our town, and the education and information infrastructure puts forth creative demands completely unlike other places. The relationship of music to political power is ground fertile enough for a whole book by itself!

But the best part is: I don't HAVE to live in either New York OR LA!

I think maybe I'll go pour myself a fat martini, plop down in front of CNN, and say: "Thank God I'm exactly where I am!"

CURRENT POSITIONS AND RESPONSIBILITIES

I joined the company, then called: "Soundwave" in October, 1988, after several years of freelance work. My initial position was that of staff composer, because that's mostly what I do. Over a period of time however, we decided I should adopt the official title of "Music Director" mostly because it sounded cooler, and because it wasn't immediately clear to many of our clients exactly what a "composer" was.

I still compose of course, but over the years, our music library has grown to a considerable size, and managing, cataloging, and tracking the use of the music has become more involved. Besides composing, I handle licensing paperwork, both directly with clients, and with Broadcast Music Inc (BMI), with whom our publishing firm, Waveworks Music, and I are both affiliated.

I am responsible for just about anything that involves music around here. I compose for clients who have the budget for original music, and make recommendations of library cuts for those who don't. I also compile our music into audio CDs, DVDs, data files, and internet-friendly formats. I do some custom computer programming for clients and the company, and put in some time as the company's webmaster.

One of the larger projects I have done, which seems to

be ongoing, is the program design of our library product, the Waveworks Music Library for Windows. It is essentially a piece of software on CD-ROM that contains nearly thirty hours of music files, compressed in MP3 format, and a search engine I designed and programmed, and am constantly in the process of improving and debugging. Many of our clients take the CD-ROM with them on airplanes and use it to search and select music for their current projects at their laptop computers.

The ultimate goal is to release the library as a commercial product.

I also drink a lot of coffee.

HERE'S THE FRONT HALL AT WAVEWORKS, IN MCLEAN. IT MAY LOOK NICE, BUT IT MEANS WE HAVE TO HAUL STUFF UP AND DOWN STAIRS.

Day 1 | **SEPTEMBER 2**

PREDICTIONS

- Probable staff meeting in the morning.
- Get with Harmon about "Boat" show, Music Library.
- Set up new piano/live stuff.

DIARY

Today is the day after Labor Day, time to start getting up earlier in the morning to get my kids off to school and prepare for the day. My oldest daughter just moved out yesterday into

15

her first apartment, so my wife and I are alternating between feeling proud and weird. Nonetheless, we get breakfast into the remaining two kids and launch ourselves into the day.

My commute takes about forty minutes in total. I drive from my house in Fairfax, VA to the office in McLean. This morning the roads are more crammed than usual due to the end of summer, but I still made it to work in plenty of time.

Being a musician, I actually juggle two jobs; my "day job," producing media music, and my "night job," performing music live in local venues. My band consists of myself and my guitar guy, Ken. Over the weekend, one of the instruments I use developed some sort of digital sickness, and I was forced to decide whether to sink more repair money into it, or bite on the bullet and buy a new one. I opted for the latter. Of course, doing so means that now I have to go through a learning curve with the new box, as well as set up my system to accommodate a new way of doing things. So I packed up the new instrument (a digital piano) and took it to the office with me.

Tuesday is our usual "staff meeting" day, so we gathered everyone together in the lobby to go over what was happening this week. The company has been (like everyone else) suffering from the current economic doldrums affecting the country, but (unlike many others) we have managed to survive, and business is beginning to pick up. There are several TV and radio spots on tap for this week, and some new, larger scale things coming down the pike over the next six to eight weeks.

All of these involve music, of course, but the budgets are such that it will probably come from the library. Fortunately, my own music library is among the available choices, and gets used a lot.

I usually check my email first thing in the morning. After a long weekend such as this one, the email tends to pile up. Most of it's junk of course, and I've tried filtering that stuff out, but unfortunately found that I had filtered out some mail that I really needed! So now I go ahead and look through my inbox, keeping the good stuff and trashing the ones that teach me ways to make so much money on eBay that I can quit my job, ways to become a millionaire by helping some ex-official from an African country move a large wad of cash, and ways to enhance my masculinity (and/or femininity).

I then spent the morning working on my new piano, reading the manual, figuring out how to use it with my system, and generally having way too much fun banging away on it.

After lunchtime, I had a brief meeting with Jim Harmon, the president of the company. He has worked out a deal with a new commercial music library that needs product, so I am now tasked with writing and producing a number of CDs of general purpose music for it. It's an open-ended project, so there is no specific deadline, but the goal is the turn out a new CD every four to six weeks.

The CDs will consist of probably 10-12 full-length compositions (three to five minutes in length), and several edits of each; a

60-second version, a 30-second version, and some "lifts" and alternate mixes. It can be a daunting challenge given the time frame, so what I will have to do is set up my entire system specifically to the needs of this project.

It's also going to require a lot of hard disk space, so I spent much of the afternoon backing up files to CD, and freeing up disk space. One of the things I needed to make space for was samples from my new piano. I want to use it in my studio system, but I don't want to haul it back and forth. So I have recorded samples from it, and now I'll create a clone of it in my studio instrument.

The sampling process is very time-consuming. Each sample has to not only be recorded, but edited so that dead space at the top and tail is removed, and normalized (all volume levels brought up to their maximum). Most of the rest of my day was spent doing that.

In the end, it was a day to get a lot of not-directly-musical work done. Tomorrow, I'll tackle some new composition. At least, that's the plan.

LESSONS/PROBLEMS

Among my problems is the email thing. I think I average about 70-90 junk emails per day. On weekends, it gets much worse if I don't check it daily. It's something I guess we all have to live with, unless some computer genius can find a foolproof way to *zap spam. Otherwise, computers have insinuated themselves into every part of our businesses, mine especially, and generally, we're better off for it.*

THIS IS THE RECEPTION DESK IN THE LOBBY, PRETTY MUCH THE FIRST THING YOU SEE WHEN YOU WALK IN THE DOOR.

Day 2 | **SEPTEMBER 3**

PREDICTIONS

- "Tour" coming through in the morning.
- Finish new piano program.
- Start some new music from library project.

DIARY

Well, I guess I shouldn't have mentioned my commute yesterday, because today the way into McLean was a parking *lot. It took me nearly an hour and a half from door to door.*

I picked up where I left off yesterday getting the piano samples into my other instrument and setting it up. It sounds very good, but I need to tweak the program so that it feels more like the kind of piano I like.

Around 10:30 we had a "tour" of one of our current clients bringing a potential new one to show the place, so we did a bit of a dog-and-pony show in all the rooms. We do this quite often to let new people know what we are and what we do. Almost everyone who comes through and takes a look in my room says: "Oh, YOU'RE the one who has all the FUN around here!" I can't really deny it.

After the tour, I started setting up the "orchestra" for the new library project. I have a lot of good orchestral samples in my collection, but they're all recorded differently. Some are small sections that were miked very close in a dry room; others are large groups in big halls, etc. etc. The trick here is to find the instruments that most closely fit together sonically so as to sound like a whole orchestra all in the same room. The easiest way to do this would be to buy one of the newer orchestral sample libraries like the Vienna Symphonic or the Quantum Leap collection, but they're $3000-$4000!! At rates like that, they should be offering 0% financing and a complimentary CD player!

So I began assembling my virtual orchestra. I usually start with strings, which tend to be the workhorses of an orchestra, and

THIS IS THE MAIN LOBBY AT WAVEWORKS, WHERE WE HOLD OUR WEEKLY STAFF MEETINGS.

work outward from there. As I go, I will put together combinations of instruments and write little short test pieces to see how they work together. The next thing is to place them within the sonic field properly. In an orchestra, the violins are placed to the left of the conductor, violas to the center-right, and cellos and basses more to the right. Some sample collections actually record the musicians "in place," but these tend to be the more expensive ones, and the jury is still out over which is better.

So I started experimenting with sonic placement and wrote a couple short string pieces to work with. The stereo image was starting to work pretty well, and it was getting late, so I saved my data, and prepared to head home (in the rain again).

Tomorrow, I'll work on a new composition (for real, not a test).

LESSONS/PROBLEMS

I have been working with strings first, and they sound pretty good. But the only way to make this whole thing work is not to combine my "best" strings with my "best" brass and woodwinds, etc. The trick is to make all these things work in context with each other. If they don't, it's often hard to tell which one (if not both) is the real culprit. It takes a lot of testing and tweaking.

Day 3 | **SEPTEMBER 4**

PREDICTIONS

- Continue working on new "orchestra."
- Finish at least one new library composition.
- Do some work on the band's CD.

DIARY

OK, today is the day I get some real musical work done. I have my new string section in place, so I'm going to get to work on a strings-centered composition.

This is all part of an ongoing project to create orchestral music for a new music library based out of New York, and the idea is to deliver a CD of music every four to six weeks. Ramping up is always the hard part, because you have to develop a methodology for production. Since this particular project involves all orchestral sounds, once a good virtual orchestra is in place, the methodology will not change much, and new music will flow out at an increasing pace.

At least, that's the theory.

I closed my door, and began to go into my "composition state." Since this is a strings-centered composition, I began by fooling around with a set of "sordini," or muted, violins. A muted section produced a very silky sound that is kind of melancholy, and so the first thing to come out was a little pattern of descending chords that repeated.

The feeling that began to come across was reminiscent of a scene from a kind of romantic mystery film, so I tried to imagine such a thing. The main melody came in on full, non-muted violins, supported by a harp on the bottom. It conjured up visions of a country house in Britain somewhere overlooking the ocean. Very romantic.

I began to introduce the mystery part by bringing in a modulation with a full string section playing in tremelando, lending a sort of "chill-wind" kind of air to the piece. Now this is getting kind of fun.

I then reintroduced the descending chords that started the piece, but this time on a piano, and that gives us not only a change that maintains interest, but the piano sounds distant, and a little spooky. The main melody then wraps around it with fuller strings, and some French horns.

I ended the piece with a return to the same descending string pulse that we began with, leading into a mysterious suspended chord ending, with those chilly string tremelandos again.

Now it's time to mix. Using MIDI instruments, a piece like this can be created with one or two (good) instruments. In my case, I use a Kurzweil K2500 sampler/synth and a Kurzweil Micro-Piano. I can listen to how the piece is coming along directly out of the instruments, but in the end, I want to separate the "orchestral" parts, strings, horns, piano etc., and treat them each a little differently, to get them placed within the sonic field the way I want, and give the whole thing the depth and dimension one would expect from an orchestra.

To do this, I transfer each part to two-tracks (stereo) of my recorder, which is an Akai DPS-16, a combination hard-disk recorder/mixer/effects processor. In this case, there are 10 tracks used. Once transferred, I get a general balance of instruments first, and save it to the recorder as a "scene," or a snapshot of where the faders are, and what EQs and effects settings I have for each channel.

Then I lock the recorder to the computer and begin mixing. The computer records the fader movements as I go, and I can go in and edit any one of them individually if I need to. After several takes of mixing, concentrating on certain sections at a time, the violins first, then the cellos and basses, then the horns, etc., I'm happy with the mix, and I then record the entire automated mix to two empty tracks in the recorder.

From there, I then save the final two-track master as a WAV file to a shared disk, and transfer it to my computer. Then I save the entire multitrack audio file to disk, and back it up, along with the two-track master, the original MIDI sequence file, and the sample set from the Kurzweil, onto a CD-ROM.

So I have been in this trance all day, and I look at the clock and it's after 4:00pm. That's not bad. We now have a new composition, finished and backed-up, and ready to send off to New York (although we're not going to do that until we are at least close to a finished CD). And I even have a bit of time left to play with some parts for a CD I'm producing for my band.

Tomorrow, I expect to work a bit on expanding the "orchestra" to include more brass and woodwinds, and perhaps I can get another piece done as well.

LESSONS/PROBLEMS

The strings are beginning to work together well. I'm getting good dimension out of them, and the French horns I added fell right into place within the tonal spectrum. I still need to get them placed in the stereo field a little better, but it's coming.

HERE IS ONE OF THE PRO TOOLS SUITES AT WAVEWORKS.

Day 4 | **SEPTEMBER 5**

PREDICTIONS

- Continue working on new "orchestra."
- Possibly write a new piece.

DIARY

Today the plan of attack is to start adding brass samples to my existing strings collection and see how well they match up. The first thing I did was start working on a general *combination of brass instruments (trumpets, trombones, and French horns) and started spreading them out within the stereo field.*

The ones I was picking out were pretty bright and powerful, so I began to digress from my initial mission, and started matching them up with some orchestral percussion, again playing with the stereo image as I went. It started to sound pretty good, and I wrote a little short test piece, and saved the file. OOOPS! It's already 126MB, and I only have 128MB of space in my Kurzweil.

You can never have too much memory or disk space, particularly when working with samples and audio files. What I'm going to have to do is develop two sets of samples for each instrument group, one with the full-length samples for final transfer to disk, and one with the same sounds, but cut way down so that I can get the whole "orchestra" into the machine to compose with.

Herein lies the rub: I could simply buy one of the newer orchestral sample libraries, and there are several, that are meticulously recorded, some in 24-bit/96kHz quality, and have the sample quality and recorded ambiance I need for this project, or for that matter, many projects to come. But these products cost three to four thousand dollars, and there is really no guarantee that they will have everything I need.

And I don't have the three or four thousand anyway, so the question is moot. I need to search through my existing sample library (which totaled over four thousand dollars itself) for the right sounds and then I have to create the ambiance from scratch. This, folks, is why they call it "art."

Well, here's the trick to digital samples: They don't sound like the real thing, they ARE the real thing. A digital sample of a hit on a tympani drum IS a "real" tymp ... BUT, it's a tymp recorded at a specific time, under specific conditions, and with all those factors bound into the sound.

One could record a tympani hit in a large room, and you could never make it sound like it was recorded in a small room. And vice-versa; you can record such a hit in a small room, and try to make it sound like it's in a large hall by adding reverb to the sound, and that will help, but the reverb you use will add depth and dimension, but when you combine that with, say, a string section recorded in a large hall, that already has the ambiance of that hall built in, you find that the ambiance of the strings is totally different than the ambiance of the tymp that you processed to sound large. The two don't quite mix!

This is going to be tricky.

LESSONS/PROBLEMS

Well, of course, the lesson here is that creation of a realistic orchestra is a tougher nut to crack than just having a collection of good orchestral sounds. When we listen to fine orchestral recordings, we're listening to a bunch of people, in the same room at the same time, playing music. That's the signature of orchestral sound. And that's what we have to imitate.

The other thing to bear in mind is the budget! I don't have three or four grand to spend, so I have to make this happen within my limited means.

Day 5 | **SEPTEMBER 8**

PREDICTIONS

- *Continue working on orchestral samples.*
- *Work at home on new studio.*

DIARY

Today is Monday. This is the day out of each week when I go in to the office for half of the day, and then go work in my home studio the other half. I have a duplicate set of equipment there, so I can take files I'm working on to disk and take them home, or just send them over the net. Often I'll work on a score at the office, finish it at home, and send it back to our main server by FTP for one of the audio guys to use in a sweetening session. Ain't computers wonderful?

I went in at 9:00 am, the usual time. Did some paperwork, and some more orchestral sample work, mostly just cleaning up and backing up of what I did yesterday. But knowing I'm leaving at noon, I didn't get into any time-consuming projects. Noon rolled around soon enough, and I packed up and left for home.

Today, I'm not exactly working IN my home studio, but more ON it. I'm in the process of constructing a new workspace in my basement that will serve as a studio, screening room, and home theater.

33

The first thing I did was build two double walls between the furnace room and the studio space, and I insulated them nice and thick to isolate the room from noise. Now I have the drywall work finished, I have wiring run (and tested) to the front speaker jacks, I've put up speaker mounts, and finished painting the main room. Next week I have carpet coming in, so I'm rushing to finish painting the smaller room that I use as an office.

Once the carpet is in, then I start putting up acoustic material around the main room. That will consist of one-inch thick fiberglass panels covered with felt and custom cut to the sizes I need. Once that's done, I'll just need to plug in the electronics. Sounds simple, huh?

The electronics are actually going to be the easy part. The center of the system is a DVD recorder, a Phillips DVDR 985. It's a good multi-function machine that can record and play back DVDs, DVD+RWs CDs, and CD-RWs, plus it can lock to time code. It also has a digital 5.1 audio output, so one cable plugged into the main amp is all it takes.

Everything else will go directly into the DVDR, the computer audio and video, my instrument mixer, and any video devices.

After a full day of painting, I'm ready to call it quits. Tomorrow, I'm back in the office.

LESSONS/PROBLEMS

Generally, this home studio project is going well, but SLOWLY. Everything has to be done in a specific order, clearing the space, doing the construction work, wiring, testing, painting, carpeting, and finally acoustics. Any snag in any process and the project grinds to a halt.

Day 6 | **SEPTEMBER 9**

PREDICTIONS

- *Staff meeting.*
- *Continue working on new "orchestra."*
- *New library composition (?).*

DIARY

Tuesday Morning. We had our weekly staff meeting at 9:15, and went over current projects that are in-house, upcoming things over the next few days or weeks, and whatever equipment might need some repair work.

After the meeting, I returned to my lair and got back onto orchestra samples. I have to admit I'm getting frustrated. I'm trying to create a new orchestra with a lot of old material. Most of it isn't bad, but it's a hodge-podge of sounds that were not recorded with any consistency of sound. I'm starting to really put a new eye on my finances to see if I can afford to take the plunge into a whole new system. If I do, I'll need to buy a new computer as well as the software. My current one would not be able to handle the load.

So it's a major investment, and it could pay for itself just in the amount of time it saves me trying to make these old samples do new tricks.

In electronic orchestration, you often find yourself living in the "Hell of too many options." You can have, and use, any sound

37

that exists, in conjunction with any other sound that exists, and create something wonderfully new. But such freedom can mean chaos if you don't determine the limits you are working within. My client in New York wants a lot of orchestral music and that determines the limitations of the sonic palliate I have to create.

In the digital world, you can have a violin if you want it, or a tympani (should that be "tympanus" if you're talking about just one, sort-of like "martini"?), or the crash of a piano falling out a six-story building, if that's what you want. You simply load it up.

But to create an effective digital "orchestra" means careful matching of instrument sound, making sure you have the expressions you need, and creating the "sound space" in which the orchestra performs. That's very difficult to do with samples taken from many different sources.

I write these things at the same time as I contemplate buying a multi-thousand-dollar package of hardware and software to solve my current problem. It's going to cost around $5000 in total. Ouch.

LESSONS/PROBLEMS

The problem is, as it has been, the creation of a realistic orchestra. I think I've made my decision. Now I have to find the money and do it so that not a lot of time gets wasted.

Day 7 | **SEPTEMBER 10**

PREDICTIONS

- More "orchestra" work.
- New Music.
- Work with band tonight.

DIARY

Traffic is still horrendous! This time I left a few minutes early and managed to make it to the office only a few minutes late.

I have been pouring over my finances lately. This music library project has convinced me that the time has come for a major upgrade. It's going to be expensive, but that's the cost of doing business in the modern age.

I am justifying this by the reality that I need to stay competitive, and this is where the business is going. I can't wait until I'm the last guy on the block to have the new tools everybody else is jumping on. And it's not going to get cheap until something better supersedes it.

So, onward and upward. This means a major system upgrade, and the entire science project that goes along with it. Oh, joy!

Otherwise, the day went pretty much normally. I spent most of the day editing several pieces I have earmarked for the library. The format of the thing is like this: each composition has to have a full-length version of three to five minutes, a 60-

second, 30-second, and 15-second edit, and perhaps some alternate mixes. I took the first three pieces, a "fantasy" (a sort of Hollywood-ish, grand-sweep sort of bit), a "romance" (a delicate and sentimental thing), and a piece based on old English and Irish folk tunes (which is a bit "Lord of the Rings"-ish), and did the editing that was needed. I still have several more things in the can to work on, so I have enough to satisfy my client should he begin to get anxious.

I use a very widely available but fabulous program called: "Cool Edit," from Syntrillium Software. It's downloadable from the internet, and it has virtually every audio tool anyone could need for $49. If you use a Windows PC for audio, this is the one to get.

All the things people used to win Grammies for are essentially built in to software like this. Fine-level editing, compression (where you can design your own compressors) reverberation and delay effects, time stretching, cross-fading, etc. etc. etc., the list just goes on. Thank God for this stuff. I would have to get a REAL JOB otherwise!

LESSONS/PROBLEMS
The lesson here, I think, is that there is so much fabulous technological stuff available for the creation of music that it seems almost impossible to create bad music.

The problem is: It can still be done.

THIS IS THE "OFFICIAL" PHOTO OF THE ELECTRONIC PHILHARMONIC, WITH THE CAPTAIN AT THE HELM.

Day 8 | **SEPTEMBER 11**

PREDICTIONS

- *Reflect on the meaning of this day.*
- *Consider the future of mankind.*
- *Plan what I will get done tomorrow.*

Today is September 11th. I have recently been advised by my publisher to keep personal observations to a minimum.

Well, that one is a little tough today. Because regardless of how we use technology, what sort of electronic trickery and tools we employ in the creation of music, it's still all about the music. And music is a product of, and a producer of, personal emotions. This day is a particularly emotional one.

So I'm going to present you with some unabashed personal observations (sorry about that, Garth).

I drove in to work this morning, as I did that morning, and it was such a beautiful morning that I left my radio off and just enjoyed the commute into town. It was a little strange.

After 9/11/01 happened, we all felt our world had changed. I found myself in a very changed musical world. The first assignment that came my way after that event was to compose music for a video that was part of the memorial service at the Pentagon. I felt honored and daunted. Other 9/11-themed projects were to follow, too many I felt, but they came.

The Pentagon Memorial, however, was the first, and it was only a few weeks after the event. The video guys handed me a tape, and I closed the door behind me and got to work. It was, quite literally, the hardest assignment I have ever had.

I tried to play music that felt appropriate, but it was either too sad, or too innocuous. Nothing I could come up with was right. Had this been a movie about a terrorist attack, it would be all action, romance, suspense, intrigue, and of course, the good guys would win in the end. This was no movie. It had to be treated with a proper level of respect.

And, frankly, I was not handling things well. I began to wonder if I would even be able to do the job.

Then I found myself playing a little piano theme from my second piano concerto (yes, I have done two of them). It's the very end of the last movement, and it's a hymn. I finished the concerto in 1995, and gave the ending piece the title: "A Hymn for Reason." I always felt mankind would be better off if we developed a higher level of respect for reason, for logic, but I had not imagined that the point would ever be driven home in the manner it was.

It's a very simple, almost old-fashioned gospel chord structure, but it reminded me of some old Anglican themes I had heard while working on another piece for another client. It carried with it a sense of loss, deep, and heavy, and yet throughout the piece, there is an underlying aura of hope, and triumph in the end. It was right.

And it was already done. I was in no shape at that time to create something new. The event was too recent, and I wasn't prepared.

So I adapted that theme to the video. It was not easy, but it was at least possible. I would create for a bit, stop, get myself back together, create, stop, recover, etc. until it was done.

We married it to the video, and that was that. I know it was hard on all of us at that time. But we did what we could, and what was right.

In truth, today passed for me rather unremarkably, for which I am today thankful. I began a new composition, which is an almost blatant rip-off of stuff from Beethoven, but damn, it's fun!

LESSONS/PROBLEMS

Well, the problem is this: mankind will probably cure cancer, AIDS, and the common cold, end poverty, and illiteracy, return the to moon, visit the planets, and even perhaps break the light-speed barrier and set foot on planets around the distant stars.

But we will do all these things long before we ever stop killing each other over religion.

I think there's a lesson in there somewhere.

Day 9 | **SEPTEMBER 12**

PREDICTIONS

- More "orchestra" work.
- New Music.
- Work with band tonight.

DIARY

Got to work at the usual time. Lisa, one of our marketing folks, says the series of spots for the USO she's been working on is a "go." They'll probably start shooting next week, but the music and post work probably won't happen for another four to five weeks.

So the most productive thing I can do right now is create some more music for the library project. I've decided to upgrade my entire system, which is going to be expensive, but the time has come. It will involve a new main computer, a huge package of orchestral software, and some upgraded sequencer software. I currently use an old version of Cakewalk for purely MIDI work, Cakewalk Pro Audio 9 for audio + MIDI work, and Cool Edit 96 for audio editing and processing. All these products are a number of years old and, while still useful, lack the more advanced capabilities of their next-generation counterparts.

I'll probably start ordering stuff next week, and it will filter in over a period of weeks to be set up, tested and debugged as I go. In the meantime though, there's music to be made.

HERE IS A SHOT OF THE MAIN MUSIC RIG AT WAVEWORKS.

I have been tending to bounce back and forth between programming and composing lately, but since I have decided to upgrade the system, the programming part is not so important anymore, and getting some new music done is taking the top spot on the priorities list.

My client with the music library is asking for classical and orchestral music mostly, so I loaded up my new strings and began composing a piece in the style of Beethoven, with lots of darkness and passion, and parts that would put blisters on the players fingers (if I was using players).

As I wrote, it began to sound like the Seventh, beginning with three big full-section tuttis, and then the violins come in to begin a fast fugue-like melody, with the violas coming in chasing them, cellos and basses following suit, thereafter.

This batch of strings works well for this kind of thing. The attacks are nice and clean, and there is plenty of "rosin" in the bowing.

After the main body of the piece was about 90% done, I added some orchestral percussion to heavy the whole thing up. Now it sounds like Beethoven!

Even though the entire piece only turned out to be about two and a half minutes in length, by the time I finished composing and mixing, it was after 3:00pm. Time flies when you're having fun! That's not bad though, that still allowed me a couple hours to do the editing I needed to do.

By five I have the piece more-or-less put to bed, but I always take new music home with me to play it on other stereo systems and make sure the sound translates well between them. So I burned it onto a CD and hit the road.

Tonight the band is working, and tomorrow we have two jobs to play, one right after another, starting at 11:00am. Sunday morning, I plan to collapse.

LESSONS/PROBLEMS

I am anxious to get the new system and software up and running so that I have a good, consistent orchestra to work with, but the existing stuff sounds good anyway. It mostly just doesn't have the dimension I like to hear in an orchestra recording. But there's no sense beating myself up over it. The new stuff will be in soon enough.

Day 10 | **SEPTEMBER 15**

PREDICTIONS

- Work at home.
- Carpet coming in for the home studio.

DIARY

Today is the day I usually go into the office for a half-day, then come home to work in my home studio, but this morning I have the installers coming to put the carpet in, so I have to deal with that. I set up my equipment in the family room so that I could do some music work while they were doing their thing.

Around 11:00am, I got a call from the carpet place. The manufacturer was supposed to send them two rolls of carpet to cover the space, but they only sent one! Since I cannot do anything else to the space until that carpet gets in, I asked them if they had enough to at least do the main room, and the office and stairs could wait. Yes, they were able to do that, so they sent the guys over.

They got there around noon and began their work by measuring and saying that they didn't have enough carpet to even get the main room the way it had originally been planned. My day was not going well at this point, so I called the carpet place and put them in touch with the installers to

THIS IS A NICE WIDE SHOT OF THE ELECTRONIC PHILHARMONIC, WHICH IS NOT ONLY A DANDY PLACE TO MAKE MUSIC, BUT IT'S GREAT FOR WATCHING "STAR WARS".

work the thing out. They figured out alternate way of cutting the carpet so that the main room was covered, and we'll just deal with the rest later. Whew!

I got back to some music work upstairs. I played back the "Beethoven" piece on my stereo. The low end sounds a little tubby. I'll have to put a high-pass filter on it when I get back to the studio tomorrow. Generally, though, it comes across pretty well.

In order to make sure my home studio matches my work, I had to bring the new samples I had been working on home and save them to the drive in my system. I also loaded them up and played them over the home speakers. They're not bad, but the new software is still the way to go, even if it is $3000.

I had to make some phone calls to move some money around in preparation for the "big buy," and spent some time online, looking at computer configurations. I finally settled on a Dell system, a 2.8 GHz P-4 with a gig of RAM, a 120-GB hard drive, and a DVD/CD-RW burner. The price comes to about $1600. I remember when I bought my first computer, and AT&T model 6300, with not ONE, but TWO floppy disk drives, and it ran at a spiffy 8 MHz! I paid $3000 for it at the time, and it was a boat anchor within a couple years.

The new system should handle the software well. The library I'm getting to the Quantum Leap Symphonic Orchestra sample set, and it has a huge collection of samples, 68 GB in all on 16 DVD-ROMs. The samples are all 24-bit resolution. The whole recording approach is a little different too.

The players were recorded in a concert hall with three simultaneous miking setups, close-mikes, stage-mikes, and hall mikes. When the samples play back on an included software sample player, the user can adjust the relative volumes of the three mike schemes to "position" the listener in the stereo field. When the sample stops playing, a sample of the natural concert hall ambience is triggered, rather than to add artificial reverb.

Around 4:00pm, the carpet guys finished and gave me their paperwork. The store will call me to set up another appointment to finish up.

LESSONS/PROBLEMS

Well, with any sort of renovation thing involving contractors, there will be problems, and today was no exception. But the main room is now carpeted, and that means I can start installing the acoustic wall treatments. That's the last major step in the construction process.

All of this pain will definitely produce gain, though, and it's all part of the process of staying on top of the creativity, and therefore business, curve.

THIS IS THE ENTIRE GANG AT WAVEWORKS, ARLINGTON, EXCEPT I'M AWOL FOR SOME REASON THAT I CAN'T ENTIRELY RECALL.

Day 11 | **SEPTEMBER 16**

PREDICTIONS

- Staff meeting.
- Clean up and re-edit the "Beethoven" piece.
- Configure, order new computer.

DIARY

We had our regular staff meeting around 9:30. Some new

work is coming down the pike, but most of it is still several weeks away.

The first order of business was to go ahead and put in the order for the new computer, which may get here by the end of the week, but I don't look for it until next week. I'm going to get it up and running and tested before I order the software.

The new "Beethoven" piece works better now that some of the low end has been reduced. One of the things I like about my editing software (Cool Edit by Syntrillium Software, recently bought by Adobe) is that you can create your own filters just by drawing them. You can boost or cut any frequency range as radically or a subtly as you wish. That's what I did with this piece. I drew a subtle slope at the low end that gradually became steeper as it approached the very low end. The result was that the rest of the frequencies were more in the open, and that helped create "air" in the piece.

After working on that, I then had to apply the same filter to the edited versions of the piece, which didn't take long.

OK, it's time to go shopping! I had to order the new computer from Dell. Being that it's Tuesday, it will probably get in early next week, but it's entirely possible it could make it in by Friday. I logged onto Dell's site and picked out the base unit, customized it to my specs and put in the order. The whole thing came to a bit over $1600. I always feel a little drained after buying something new. Of course, the software will cost $3000. I'll probably have to lie down after that one.

So the computer is a done deal. The software, however, I'm going to order later. There are several orchestral packages out there, all equally expensive, and I need to make sure I'm going to get the right one. So I got onto the net and went to Soundsonline.com. These are the guys selling the Quantum Leap package ($2999). I read over all the specs for probably the tenth time, and listened to the demos (which are pretty impressive).

Then I went to the Ilio site. These guys sell the Vienna Symphonic Library, a very similar package. The main difference between the two is that the Vienna collection was recorded in a specially-built anechoic (dry) studio, while the QL collection was recorded in a concert hall, and uses the acoustics of the hall instead of allowing for the addition of reverb after the fact. There is also an older orchestral collection from Miroslav Vitous that was actually the first of these huge orchestral packages. There are a couple others that specialize in strings, or brass, etc. I listened to the demos from all of them, and they all sound very good, but still the QL collection sounded best to my ears. So, OK, the decision was made.

I chatted with Ian, one of our audio guys, for a bit about the whole upgrade and sample collection thing. He has the "mini" version of the Miroslav collection, a more budget-conscious edition, and he would bring it in sometime for me to fool with. That could be fun, but I think I'm still going to run with the QL package.

I generally check my email several times a day, and so around 3:30 I did so. It contained the usual mosh of junk, and most of the time there isn't anything real in the box. But I look through it anyway, just to make sure I'm not letting some real email get past me. Nestled in among it all was an invoice from Earthlink. That's funny. I used to use Earthlink for my band's site, but moved to another provider several months ago. Earthlink does, however, host our company's website, but I still shouldn't be getting the invoice.

Well, well! I opened the email and found a bill for $26,046.20! Hmmm. They had tried to automatically charge my credit card and had been declined. I'm not surprised. The charges were for Sept 13 thru Oct 12; $19.95 for hosting, and Sept 12 thru Sept 12 (?); a web bandwidth charge of $0, and then another bandwidth charge, also for Sept 12 of $26,026.25! Twenty-Six grand for one day worth of bandwidth? Seems a tad pricey.

So I printed it out and took it down to Brenda, our accountant and the person who should be getting the bills. She tried to call Earthlink at the number on the invoice, and got immediately lost it the voicemail menu system from Hell! Not a human being to be found. My guess is that the $26K bill was the result of similar automation.

She couldn't get anywhere, so I got onto their site to see what I could do. They have a customer support chat system, reportedly featuring "live" human beings on the other end. I got onto that and a minute or so later, someone greeted me and asked how to help. I typed in the story of the 26K bill and hit "enter." There was a fairly pregnant pause before the support person got back to me, but after a minute or so, the message came: "Can you please give me 10 minutes to check on this?" "OK" I said.

After close to 20 minutes, it was 5:00, and I typed in a note that I couldn't wait any longer, and gave them the number to call us. End of chat, end of day.

The saga, I'm sure, is to be continued.

LESSONS/PROBLEMS

This day was a reminder of the promise AND folly of the internet. The "up" side is that I can surf around and find info I want about any piece of music gear or software I'm interested in, and even listen to how it sounds in order to make up my mind. I can order stuff on the spot and have it delivered right to my door within a day or so. Wonderful! This is how I do my Christmas shopping anymore.

And then there is the "down" side, and getting a bill for $26,000 certainly qualifies as one. The dependence on computers and automation, without having human beings riding herd over the whole thing, can generate a cascading series of screw-ups that leads to such laughable stuff as this.

Reminds me of a famous piece of music: "The Sorcerer's Apprentice" (starring Mickey Mouse).

HERE'S THE "OFFICIAL" PHOTO OF JIM HARMON, JIM BLOCH, AND BRENDA RAYNER, THE OWNERS OF WAVEWORKS.

Day 12 | **SEPTEMBER 17**

PREDICTIONS
- *New Music.*
- *Music editing.*
- *Deal with the Earthlink problem.*

DIARY

Got in to the office a bit late, thanks again to the traffic. The first thing I wanted to do was find out if Earthlink had contacted us. So far, no. Maybe no news is good news.

So I headed to my studio and started doing a little editing of some existing pieces for the library. Using Cool Edit, I cut two existing pieces into :60 and :30 versions. I have to do this for all the new library pieces.

While I was editing, Jim Bloch, the vice-president and our "chief science officer" came in to ask me some questions about our wireless network. Some months ago, I became a convert to and an absolute evangelist for wireless networks. I have a tablet computer, a Fujitsu ST4110, with built-in 802.11b wireless capability, and so I brought in a wireless access point and set it up on our internal network. Now I can walk around the plant and access our network or the internet from anyplace upstairs (the signal gets too weak downstairs, but I can get on if I stand in the hall beside the downstairs bathroom).

Now it seems, more and more of our clients are bringing in laptops with wireless adapters in them, and we're putting them onto our network that way. But our system uses static IP addresses, so we have to assign one to the visitor's computer as well, which is a bit of a pain.

So we now want to set up the access point as a DHCP server so that users can just walk in and get on without any fooling around. It seems like it should be easy enough, but then again, this is "computers."

So I tried to log into the access point's built-in configuration utility with my browser. It asked me for my password and I gave it, but it did not recognize it, and wouldn't let me in. After several attempts and much griping on my part, I realized that I had not yet set up a password on this access point, so it was still using the default. I tried the default password and got in.

It was then that I discovered that this is an access point ONLY, not a combination access point/router like mine at home, so it can't be setup as a DHCP server. For the time being at least, that means we'll still have to jump through some hoops to set up our clients on the wireless network.

I went down to talk to Jim about what I had found, and we looked at the Urchin statistics for our website over the last couple days. There was a huge spike in bandwidth on the day in question. Apparently one of our video guys put a Quicktime movie up on the site for one of our other engineers to access, and a robot of some sort found it and linked it to a zillion people on the net. That appears to be why we got slammed. Well, whatever happened, Earthlink should have an automatic shutdown in place to deal with such stuff. Bottom line is: we're not paying the 26 grand!

Ken called with several new dates for the band, so I got those into our main calendar, and went back to editing.

I was planning to start a new composition today, but it got to be past 4:30 in a hurry, so I just spent the rest of the day editing.

LESSONS/PROBLEMS

Oh those darn computers! So many things can go wrong in so many ways, from a simple password glitch to a website attack. You really can't foresee every possibility, because computers are supposed to open up new possibilities all the time. If they ever develop "smart" toasters that automatically log onto the internet, I'm not buying one. It would probably burn down my house!

Day 13 | **SEPTEMBER 23**

PREDICTIONS

- Recover from hurricane.
- Backup data in prep for new system.
- Try to get in some new music.

DIARY

Hurricane Isabel came roaring through the area over the last few days and spanked us all, some worse than others. Our servers went down, no surprise there, and electricity was out between midday Thursday and Monday. I had the same situation at home. So basically the last five days have dropped off the earth. Now it's time to go back and deal with the aftershocks.

On Thursday, as the storm approached, I shut down all my computers at work and home, but forgot to do the same with my laptop, which was plugged in and in standby mode. When the power hit came, it torched the battery. Damn!

Anyway today is the day to try to recover. We had a hole in our roof that we thought was fixed, but apparently not. A significant amount of water got in and soaked the carpet in the "digital pit," our room dedicated to computer file conversion and DVD production tasks. Fortunately the computers seem to have not been affected. The carpet, however, is badly mildewed.

I went into my room to assess the situation, turned on my computers and instruments, and everything worked! No disasters to recover from! I had figured that there would be little digital gremlins throughout the system, so I was mentally prepared for it. When I found there weren't any, I was ecstatic.

I then went on the net to check on a new instrument I had ordered over the weekend (and have been very anxious to get my hands on), and found it was backordered! There went my ecstasy!

I was originally intending to do some data backup work in preparation for my upcoming upgrade, but decided to do some new music instead. If the muse bites, you're bit!

I had a piece I had done a couple months ago called: "The Left Wing," kind of a takeoff of the type of theme music you hear on the popular TV show of a slightly different name. The piece is a very grand and dignified orchestra piece, with lots of sweep and scope, but it was a bit short, only 53 seconds. I decided to extend it by writing a middle interlude.

In the new middle part, I brought the orchestra down very low into a more gentle and introspective feeling, with the main melody interpreted on woodwinds, oboe first, then flute, supported by strings and harp. The whole middle ended up being only about another 50 seconds, but it serves as a nice bridge between the very grand entrance and exit.

The composition took the bulk of the day, and around 3:00pm

THE "CORE" AT WAVEWORKS. ALL AUDIO, VIDEO, DATA, AND WHATEVER MEET IN THIS ROOM.

it was done and mixed. Now it was time to edit. Each composition for this project consists of a full-length theme and :60 and :30 edits. I generally don't think in terms of time when I'm composing, I just let whatever comes out come out. So naturally each edit is a new challenge.

In this case, I cut the original piece (without the new interlude) in half and married the first four bars with the last 8 by fading the first into the second at a strategic location. It worked, and I had my :30 version.

The :60 was a bit harder. Since the original piece was only :53, I had to find a way to add some stuff to it. I didn't want to try to do a time-stretch, because even the best of them tend to make the music sound funny, with a slight hint of "underwater-ness." I was able to add a couple seconds to the head bringing the whole thing in with a cymbal roll. Then at the back end, I extended the closing crescendo with some tricky cross-fading. Voila! 59 seconds!

I now have almost enough new music for the first CD of the series. One or two new compositions and I'll have it in the can, hopefully by the end of the week.

LESSONS/PROBLEMS

There's very little in the world that can bum you out more than finding out that the new toy you bought won't arrive on time. But I at least got an ETA of three (long) weeks. Well, you gotta roll with it.

The library project is beginning to fall into place, even though I don't have to new system in and up yet. Once that's in, the next CD should be quite an improvement, and it's always good to follow something your client already likes with something that is clearly an improvement.

Day 14 | **SEPTEMBER 24**

PREDICTIONS

- Continue backups.
- Business networking meeting.
- Find out about cover for my piano.
- New Music.
- Work with band tonight.

DIARY

Today is a marketing day. My neighbor invited me to a "networking group" meeting, which is essentially a gathering of people from various businesses that get together on a regular basis to exchange referrals and possible sales leads. The group doesn't like the word "leads," but that's what much of it is.

The meeting was to take place at 11:00, so I had a little time to continue backing up my files from the old computer. The new one should be here any day.

Around 10:30, I took off for Arlington, to the Washington Suites Hotel for the meeting. My wife met me there and we went on up. There was a lunch served and about 20 or so people. This particular group is called BNI, Business Networking International, and they are apparently a fairly large club. They take in new members, hold meetings for guests and prospective members, and give seminars on business networking.

All of the "guests" were asked to stand up and give a short self introduction and a bit of a plug about what we do and who can benefit, etc. They went around the room in turns.

My business was by far the most esoteric of the group. Most of the people there were independent service professionals; there were several lawyers, a website designer, a lady who sold party favors, etc. There were also some folks who were part of small companies, generally with a small employee pool, but a few, like my wife, were with larger firms.

Most of the attendees, however, had businesses that dealt more directly with the public. There was little of what would be thought of as "B2B," which is more along the lines of what I do.

We had lunch, did our little bits, yakked a bit and exchanged business cards. I came away doubting that the group would do me much good, but it might be more valuable for my wife.

I went back to the studio, and continued my backup thing. Called Guitar Center and found out that the cover for my piano was in, so I can pick that up after work.

I had hoped to get some new music written today, but the business lunch and the process of backing up all these files ate into my time. It wasn't long before 5:00pm rolled around, and I wanted to swing by Guitar Center on my way home, so I made my way out the door on time.

HERE'S THE UPSTAIRS CONFERENCE ROOM AT WAVEWORKS, MCLEAN.

LESSONS/PROBLEMS

Going to the networking lunch was an illuminating experience, even if it doesn't seem likely to do me any particular good. Mostly it showed that there are a lot of networking opportunities like that one out there, and no doubt there are some that would be more oriented to my business. But the other side of such things is that I have been to some music oriented networking events, and they are mostly populated by people looking for work, and are hoping I can help them. In other words, everybody wants my job!

Day 15 | **SEPTEMBER 25**

PREDICTIONS

- Set up new computer.

DIARY

My new computer arrived last night, and so today I have only one expectation: to be banging away on that getting it set up and running. "Plug and play" is not the way it works around here. Every new computer requires a gar amount of jumping through hoops just to get to the starting point.

I arrived at the office about nine as usual, and hauled the two boxes upstairs. Much oooing and ahhhing accompanied my arrival, as is normal anytime someone gets a new toy. What can I say? We're all geeks.

I moved my old computer to a makeshift table (the floor, with the monitor on a chair) and opened the boxes up. The CPU was in one box, and a flat screen LCD monitor in the other. Both items are a nice, sexy black. I set up the monitor and keyboard on the desk, set the CPU into the rack cabinet underneath (sideways), and hooked them up to each other, and to the network first. I needed to get the network up first for two reasons: one, because I would need to transfer files to the new box over the network, and two, because networking a computer has always been a science project every time we have done it, so it's best to get the most painful stuff out of the way early.

This new machine is running Windows XP Pro, and I am told this version of Windows is much more stable and "easy" to use than previous ones. Uh huh. Once everything was hooked up, I fired that bad boy up.

I first came to the Win XP Setup "Wizard." It began by asking me to give the computer a unique name. I called it: "PatsDell." Then I clicked the "next" button. The computer froze.

Here I was sitting in front of my brand new computer, I perform ONE operation, and the very first time I click the mouse, the machine crashes! I start thinking this is going to be a very long day. I also find myself with lowered expectations for Windows XP.

I shut down and rebooted. The "wizard" returned at the next step. I presumed the first step had made it though OK, so I moved on. The next step was to enter TCP/IP information. I did that and hit "next."

The computer froze.

OK, now I'm angry. I shut down and rebooted again. Once again, the computer returned to the next step in the process. From that point on, it didn't freeze anymore. Perhaps it used its "intelligence" to "repair" itself. I got all the way through the process and all the way into Win XP. Halleluiah! Step one is done.

Onward to step two: networking. The first thing I did was open Internet Explorer. Wow! Without the usual hour and a half of jerking around, there it was. I was on the net! Score one for Win XP. But getting on to the internal network would be a bit more involved. I got with Jim Bloch to assign an IP address to the new computer. He did that. Then I went to Mark P, our IT guy, to create an account on the server for it. He did that.

I went back to my room and looked for the network. It was there! Score three for Win XP! OK, maybe I have been a bit harsh on Microsoft in the past but, well, the jury is still out.

Step three is the most important for me. I need to get the musical stuff working. I need to set up the MIDI interface, the audio stuff, and test it all, and all of it checks out, I'm back in business. This is why I needed the network up first. All the software and MIDI drivers are on the other computers. So I added my Fujitsu tablet as a user since most of the stuff I needed was on it. Then I copied the MIDI interface files to the new box, plugged it in and set it up.

All the instruments were already plugged into the MIDI chain, so I set up the interface, copied my sequencer program (an old version of Cakewalk) over, and launched it. It came up without a hitch, and I loaded a sequence file with a simple piano piece to test it. It played! My God! I got this far and it wasn't even noon yet!

OK, let's try some audio. I had already connected the computer's main ins and outs to the mixer, so I copied over an audio file, and played it. It worked! At this point, I'm getting scared. Things are going too smoothly! Something HAS to go wrong!

So it goes for the rest of the afternoon. I copy files and install programs, and everything goes off without a hitch. This process is going to continue for a few days, but I am officially back in business. Cool!

LESSONS/PROBLEMS

The only problem I had was being scared that everything was going too well to be true. I had never had the switch to a new computer go this painlessly before. Lessons? Well, maybe Bill Gates has finally gotten his product ready for prime time.

Well, maybe!

THIS IS A SHOT OF THE AUDIO GANG AT WAVEWORKS.

Day 16 | **SEPTEMBER 26**

PREDICTIONS

- Lots of file copying.
- MAYBE a new music piece to shake down the system.
- Test the new battery for my Fujitsu.

DIARY

I began the day by lowering my expectations for the day.
Yesterday went off so well, I figured today had to be more
problematic. It just HAD to! Fundamental laws of the universe
would have to be violated for that not to be the case.

The new battery I ordered for my Fujitsu tablet arrived today,
so I stuck it onto the computer and tried to fire it up. No luck.
Whatever is wrong is inside the computer, rather than just a
toasted battery. The good news is that my original battery is
probably OK, so I now have it and a spare. The bad news is I
still have to send the tablet back.

Today I have a lot of file copying to do. There are a lot of
programs that cannot be just copied, but have to be
reinstalled, so this is the day to do that. For the most part, I'm
going to transfer this stuff via CD-RW rather than the network
for the sake of both speed and not clogging up our network
bandwidth.

The first priority is to install Cakewalk Pro Audio 9 and all the
current files I have. Living in the age of gigantic hard drives as
I am today, I have decided that from now on, I'm going to
copy the entire CD-ROM to a location on the hard drive, and
install it from there. It uses up more room, but hey, we got
room! I can remember (at the risk of dating myself) the time
when I bought my first hard disk, and huge 20 (whole) MB
thing that I never did manage to fill up.

Now I have 120GB. That's 6000 times the amount of that first drive. Sometimes it gets pretty bizarre to realize that I can keep the text from most of the Library of Congress on my machine, and still have room for my checkbook.

The Cakewalk install went smoothly, and I tested it with a file from my band. Works well, sounds great. So far, so good. I spent much of the day copying and installing.

Now, we're beginning to get somewhere. Now I have the computer set up and networked, MIDI and audio tested, and everything in the system can talk to each other. Now it's about time to order that $3000 software package. This is the part that's scary to me, because every sample package I ever bought contained almost as much unusable stuff as good stuff. The thought of putting out $3000 for $1500 worth of usable sounds makes me nervous, especially since last night, I was browsing the latest copy of Keyboard magazine, and lo, there was an ad for the Garritan Orchestra Library, a similar product, for $250.00! OK, it got my attention.

The Garritan people are well known for their string samples, so this is clearly a high-quality package. I decided to surf over there and check it out.

The first thing to hit my eye was the fact that they were currently taking "pre-orders" for the package, due out in the "Fall." So the package is not yet available. I went to their demos page, and they said demos for the orchestra pack were "coming soon."

This is kind of an exercise in frustration. Everything is being sold before it's ready, beta-tested by the paying customer, and almost ready for prime-time by version 3.0. Don't get me started!

Five o'clock rolled around. The weekend is just about upon us, and I have to do a bunch more financial wrangling before I buy anything anyway.

LESSONS/PROBLEMS

The music business is now so inexorably tied to the software business I'm surprised I haven't yet been bought by Microsoft (Hmmm. Maybe I should look into that!) Any large-scale expansion of one's business is going to be accompanied by more than a little trepidation, especially when large amounts of cash are at stake, so I want to make sure I'm making the right decision. Of course, you can never really be "sure." Most of this, just like life, is an educated guess.

Day 17 | **SEPTEMBER 27**

PREDICTIONS

- Carpet Installation.
- Check order status.

DIARY

Today is the day I get the rest of the carpet installed in my new home studio. I knew today was going to be little more than dealing with that, and I wouldn't be able to get any musical work done since the carpet guys were going to be pounding away in my studio all day. I can make a few phone calls, though.

The installers arrived about 11:00am, and I showed them the basement. Their first question was: "is there a back door?" Answer: "no." Great expressions of disappointment followed. I can understand. A big roll of carpet is heavy! Well, sorry guys!

The installers went out to the truck to get out the carpet. Since there was no back door, they opted to do most of the major cutting out in the street before bringing it in and down the stairs.

I had ordered a Kurzweil K2661 from Musicians' Friend a week ago, and went to their website to track my order. According to their tracking, the unit was waiting to be picked up, but the tracking had not been updated since the day after I ordered it last week. I decided to call and check up on it.

79

A young lady answered after the obligatory "All of our operators are assisting other customers. Please wait ...," but it didn't take too long. I asked about the order and she put me on hold to check. She came back a few moments later to tell me that they needed confirmation that I still wanted the product.

Huh? Well, yes I still want the product, I said, and she said that was all she needed and it would ship tomorrow. OK that's pretty strange, but I gathered that sometimes when people make a large purchase of an expensive item such as this, they sometimes get buyer's remorse and then just return the item when it comes. They wanted to avoid that.

Around 4:00pm, the carpet guys finished up. It looks very good, I'm happy. Now I'm starting to feel like progress is being made, albeit slowly.

LESSONS/PROBLEMS

I have to admit I was a little taken aback by the Musicians' Friend thing. I have ordered a number of things from them before and never ran into any problems. I was also disappointed because I expected to have the instrument by now, and now I have to wait another week. Oh well. Sometimes ya just gotta roll with it.

THIS IS ONE OF THE CONFERENCE ROOMS AT WAVEWORKS WHERE WE MEET WITH CLIENTS AND WORK OUT GENERAL PRODUCTION STUFF.

Day 18 | **SEPTEMBER 30**

PREDICTIONS

- *Staff meeting.*
- *More computer setup.*
- *Get with Ian re: the USO job.*

DIARY

I got in to work about the usual time, and we did our Tuesday morning staff meeting. Business is picking up bit by bit. We all have something productive to do, so that makes us breathe a little easier.

After the meeting, I went upstairs to continue my computer setup. Everything has so far gone well, and now I have my most important stuff, the MIDI sequencers, digital audio editors, and video software in the box, tested, and working. Now it's mostly a matter of figuring out what other stuff I want to put on this computer. Getting a new one always offers the option of "cleaning house," and throwing away unneeded stuff. That's what I'm planning to do here.

One thing that will not be going onto the new system is the music library program. For some reason, I cannot get it to play the library's MP3 files from within the program. I have had the same problem on my Fujitsu Win 2000 machine, but it doesn't seem to have anything to do with the OS, because the library works fine on all the Win 2000 and Win NT machines in the house, and several of my clients have been running it on the XP machines with no problem. It seems like I am the only guy in the universe with this problem.

I talked with Ian (audio guy) a bit about the USO project. They now say they don't have the budget anymore. This isn't unusual. Many times a project will start out with a reasonable music budget, but then the realities of scripting, shooting, and *editing begin to nibble away at it. Music and final mix/sweetening are always the last steps in the process, so sometimes the only thing left of the budget by the time it gets to me are the crumbs.*

It looks like that's what is happening here. They are now searching the music libraries for some drops that may work.

So, with some free time on my hands, I decided to check up on my Musicians' Friend order. Well, what's this? It now says I have been BACKORDERED! The machine will not be in until November!

Wait a minute! When I ordered this thing, it was in stock. It seems while they were fooling around waiting for me to call them and confirm that I REALLY WANTED IT, they sold out. Now I was angry. I decided to cancel the order, and try to find one someplace else. I called them up and cancelled.

Then I started scouring the 'net for someone who had them in stock. After about an hour, no luck! What a bummer!

Finally, I stumbled upon an eBay ad from a New York company who claimed they would have them in about two weeks, and were taking pre-orders. Well, that's better than a month and a half, so I bought it.

I'm spending money as if I had it, and there's still a bunch of stuff to do.

I have to finish my home studio. That mostly involves

construction materials, all of the electronics have either been ordered of received already.

I also have to get several software packages for the new computer. One is the orchestral sample set (a huge expense), and the other is an upgrade from my current version of Cakewalk Pro Audio (v9) to Sonar, their latest and greatest audio product.

There's sure to be other little do-dads along the way that will add up to a million dollars or so. But, you know what they say: a million here, a million there, pretty soon it starts to add up to real money!

LESSONS/PROBLEMS

The MP3 problem is a real puzzlement. I can't seem to repeat it on any other system I try. I'll have to check out some user groups and find out if anyone else is experiencing this. As for other difficulties, the budget thing is a never-ending battle, and is simply part of the business. At least I have my own music library among the others, so they may still use something of mine.

As for that other problem: anybody know where I can get a real low-interest loan?

Day 19 | **OCTOBER 1**

PREDICTIONS

- More library music.
- Continue moving files between computers.
- Check out Kevin Bacon's Band.

DIARY

The morning started out relatively normal. Had breakfast with the kids and got them off to school, and Karen and I bolted for work. We made arrangements for the kids to make their own quick-and-easy dinner tonight (macaroni and cheese with a salad that they will hopefully take a couple bites of) because my wife and I are actually going out. We're going with my friend (and band partner) Ken and his wife to the Birchmere, a local music house/restaurant, to see the Bacon Brothers, Kevin Bacon's band. Our wives are more excited about this than we are, but it should be fun.

I got to work about the usual time and went upstairs to crank up my gear in expectation of another long day of file-moving and sorting. Ian, the audio guy, grabbed me in the hall and said that the USO client NOW wants to use original music. He found something he liked in the library, but it can't be made to work right all the way through all the spots, and would I talk to the guy about it.

Hmmm. Well, this is another thing that happens a lot. A client

THIS IS THE "GRAVEYARD" OF THE OLD ELECTRONIC STUFF. MOST OF IT STILL WORKS, BUT HAS BEEN SUPERCEDED BY NEWER WHIZ-BANGS. IT ALL SCREAMS "I'M NOT DEAD YET!"

will often come right down to the crunch and realize that the music needs a lot more than just an edit job to work, and there is no more time (or patience) for searching for something else. I said I would talk to him.

When he got in, Ian let me know, and while they were taking a break from sweetening, Ian introduced us.

He said he had found a piece that had the right general feeling in the beginning, but after 20 seconds or so, it went off in another direction, and they couldn't simply edit it in such a way as to work. He asked if I could create a kind of "sound-alike," and could I do it incredibly fast and cheap. It was Wednesday, and he had to walk out with all of the spots by end-of-day Friday. I threw a general range of numbers at him, and he agreed.

We went into the edit suite and had Paul showed some of the images from the spots (they had just begun editing) while we listened to the music. It was a nice warm and dignified string orchestra piece that did just about what the client said it would, worked very nicely for the first two-thirds of the spot, but then got big and bold and off the track completely. I felt I knew what he was going after, so I was going to look for the CD and get to work.

But the client then said that one of the other people he was working with heard a different piece and liked that. So we listened to it while watching the same spot. It was quite a bit different in mood, with a piano rhythm that led into a sweet but (in my view) overly "happy" feeling. This spot was supposed to be about how the USO cares for the men and women in uniform, and understands the sacrifices the make, and intends to be there for them. This piece didn't feel like that to me, or to the producer, but he wanted me to see if I could somehow combine the two ideas in some way. That's always easier said than done. I told him I would see what I could do.

I planned to focus more on the feeling of the first piece, but I could put in some piano accompaniment for the other client.

I began writing, based on the first piece, and began with strings, as that piece did. As the piece developed, I added the piano, more as an afterthought than as anything central to the music. I spent about three hours composing, and decided I would present a rough demo to the client after lunch.

Around 2:00pm, I put the demo onto a CD, and took in into Paul's room. They were still editing, but the first part of the spot was strung together. It was images from the Korean War Memorial, the bronze statues of ordinary soldiers that reside on the Mall in downtown DC. We played the music against the images. The tone now seemed a bit "sad." The piano I put in (to placate the other client who was not there) seemed to make the whole thing feel plodding.

We talked a bit about how to approach the piece, and now that I could see the images and the direction of the video, I felt I had a better handle on it than when I was just flying blind. The client also made sure to release me from any perceived obligation to use a piano (good). I went back to my room and started revisions.

From this point on, the approach would be orchestral. I began with the same strings figure as before, removed the piano entirely, and began working. A short time later, Paul brought me a tape of the rough video to work with.

There are two basic ways to approach a video like this; (one) to pre-score it, MTV-style, and let the editors cut to the music, or (two) post-score, writing the music directly against the existing video. The latter approach is the way I work most often, and that's the way it was in this case. The video I was working with was not finished, but most of the images were in, and the timing (critical) was correct.

I worked on the piece until close to 5:00, and had something that was getting close. I went in the check in with Paul, but the client had gone for the day. Fair enough. I decided to do the same. So I saved all my data and left for home. It's always good to "sleep on it" if you have the luxury of time.

LESSONS/PROBLEMS

The problems I face in this business generally are related to the incredible shrinking budget and this one is no exception. I am down to just a couple days to get this thing done and put to bed, as opposed to the original five days proposed. This makes the job harder, but it also provides the silver lining of forcing the client to make clear decisions on the music rather than to micro-manage it. There is always a yin and yang to these things.

HERE'S ANOTHER VIEW OF THE ELECTRONIC PHILHARMONIC WITH ALL THE INSTRUMENTS IN PLACE.

Day 20 | **OCTOBER 2**

PREDICTIONS

- Work on the USO music.
- Work with the band in the evening.

DIARY

Last night my wife and I went out with a couple friends to the Birchmere (music hall/restaurant) to see the Bacon Brothers. It *was a lot of fun. The band was quite good, but I did feel that Kevin Bacon should not quit his day job (I don't think he's planning to).*

My day job began by picking up where I left off yesterday. The client was not yet in, but Paul had a revised video for me. The changes in the video had no real effect on the music, there were just a few new images replacing some black holes in the first one. I played the piece against it. It felt pretty good, so I continued working on it, expanding the orchestration a bit.

The client arrived about 11:30 and I took the new piece into Paul's room. We played it against the picture a couple times, and the client remarked that he wanted it to get much bigger at a certain place in the video. That wasn't the impression I had gotten from our initial conversations. I had thought that he didn't want the piece to get big like the library piece it was modeled after.

He played the library piece and at the point he was talking about, it did indeed get rather big. Well OK. I can do that. I went back to my room to revise.

The next few hours were spent in revision, and the piece was coming nicely. I was still puzzled how I could have gotten the wrong impression about what he wanted. Well anyway, the piece was now getting nice and big, bigger than I thought necessary, but it sounded pretty good.

The client was in and out most of the day, so around mid-

afternoon, I gave Paul a CD with the revised music on it to play for the client whenever he got in.

A bit later, he did get in, and he and Paul came to my room to talk. The piece had gotten, well, "too big."

Hmmm. Now what? It appeared that the client wanted to hear a lot of bottom end in the piece, very deep cellos and double-basses filling it up, and this appeared to be what he meant by "big." I have made the piece "big" by bringing the whole thing up to a crescendo at the important spot, with brass, woodwinds, and percussion.

The client apologized for our miscommunication, as did I, and I set to work to get the piece done. Out goes the brass, percussion, winds, harps, etc. In comes a double-bass section adding a lower octave to the existing bass. All the low-end strings then get pulled up in the general mix.

It was close to end of day now, and I played it for the client. He liked it. Alright! I gave the 60-second version to Paul to mix into the spot. Tomorrow, I'll edit the whole thing down to the 30, 15, and 10-second versions.

Tonight, I have a gig with my band, so I'm getting out of here.

LESSONS/PROBLEMS

My clients are generally very "visual" people. They think in terms of images and movement. Music is very important, or course, but most video producers don't really know what they want musically, they just know it when they hear it. Communication between me and the client is vital. But often I have to interpret their ideas based on their very "visual" descriptions of what they want. I don't always hit it on the head right away. Sometimes, a little back-and-forth is the only way to nail it down, particularly with a new client (like this one) whose tastes and habits I have not yet learned.

Day 21 | **OCTOBER 3**

PREDICTIONS

- Finish USO music.
- Order new software.
- Work with the band in the evening.

DIARY

Got in to work at the usual time and went straight to the coffee machine. Mornings after a late-night band gig are always a little slower than others. Fortunately, the client is happy with the music now, so it's all just a matter of doing a few nips and tucks to fit it into different timings.

The other thing on my agenda is to order new production software. I have been using Cakewalk and Cakewalk Pro Audio, which are both fine programs and I've been using them for years. But I'm going to need some additional capabilities now.

I need tighter integration of video and audio/MIDI sync within the computer. Some of that is addressed simply by the increased speed and power of this new computer, but I also need the ability to use software plug-ins, such as virtual instruments and signal processors. Cakewalk has a new product out now with all these things, called: "Sonar."

Over the last few years, Cakewalk has been moving its products closer to the audio side of production, and while not necessarily moving "away" from the MIDI sequencing end of things, treating MIDI more as a nice feature rather than the main focus of the software.

That's OK by me, I need multi-track audio. But when I'm working on a project in it's earlier (MIDI) stages, I still go back to me trusty Cakewalk version 1.02. It's fast, efficient, optimized for MIDI, and uses a whopping 412K ("K"!) of memory.

After getting a bit of coffee into me, I got onto the 'net and ordered the upgrade to Sonar. That done, I went to work on the alternate versions of the USO spot.

Paul gave me the finished spots first thing in the morning, and with the :60 finished, I started plowing into the :30. It's always easier to cut something long into something shorter than it is the other way around. And since I'm editing the MIDI files themselves, rather than audio, I can use things like increasing or decreasing the tempo in places, stretching or shrinking individual notes, etc.

The :30 was relatively easy. It began with the string figure, but the :60 version repeats the entire passage. In the :30, I removed the repeat, and went right to the closing chord.

The :15 was a bit trickier. I had to further cut the opening string figure in half, and attach the closing chords, but it came up a little short. Here's where I used the tempo change trick.

In the :10, I simply took the first five notes, and made the last one conclude on the tonic.

The editing process took about three hours. I then put the finished audio files on our main server, and Ian was able to get them from there and place them into the spots.

Once I finish a project, I go through a backup routine to make sure I can find everything that went into the project in case the client comes back a year from now and needs a revision, which happens quite often. I have a file-folder system on one of the computers in which I keep a folder for the finished audio, one for the MIDI sequence data, one for the samples and programs used to create the music, and a folder for paperwork.

All that data stays on the computer's hard drive until I build up enough to have about 600MB or so, then I'll burn it onto a CD-ROM, with the folder structure, and then I have my main backup. I may switch over to DVD-RW now that I have one, and that will compact things greatly, but still I have three years worth of project data on 15 CDs, so it isn't all that urgent.

Once a year, I go through all the audio files from the previous year's projects, and after making sure they're backed up, I will then replace the WAV files with MP3s of them, in order to save disk space, but still be able to reference the audio if I need.

OK, the project is in the can, backup is done, paperwork is done and handed off to Kim. I have a band gig tonight, so I'm puttin' the hammer down.

LESSONS/PROBLEMS

This was a relatively easy day. Most of the difficulties with the project were handled beforehand, and this was mostly finishing up, and closing out the project. The biggest problem of this day is that, being an "instant-gratification" kind of guy, I now find myself having to wait a few days for my new software to get here. Well, the weekend is upon me. I'll muddle through.

Day 22 | **OCTOBER 6**

PREDICTIONS

- Go into office in the morning.
- Sonar might be in but I doubt it.
- Order Garritan strings.

DIARY

This was my day to go in to the office for half the day, and then work at home. There wasn't much on the agenda today, so I decided to get on the 'net and order the Garritan strings collection. I had been toying with the idea for a while, because they are wonderful strings, but I was hesitant because I also fully intend to order the Quantum Leap orchestral collection, which has fabulous strings as well. And the two might not match up well when used together.

Well, I decided to take that chance, simply because the Garritan collection is so good. I got on the 'net and placed the order.

While I was surfing anyway, I decided to check my current American Express bill, so I logged on to the Amex site, and took a look at my bill. My jaw hit the floor!

I have been spending money with some abandon lately, but this just couldn't be right! I looked at the recent charges and saw that Earthlink had billed my card for over $3000 of

99

website bandwidth charges for my company. I had thought we had that thing straightened out after that $26,000 bill. Apparently not.

I printed out a copy of my statement and went down to talk to Brenda about it. She said that they had gotten with Earthlink and worked out a deal for the bandwidth. Since it was mostly an accident that caused the entire world to hit our site, they dropped most of the bill, and negotiated a new charge, which we agreed to pay. But it looked like they then charged my Amex for the new bill. Man!

They spent the rest of the morning trying to get a hold of Earthlink again. I called American Express and cancelled my existing card, and opened a new account.

Around noon, I headed for home. I had gotten a call over the weekend from the fabric store where I had ordered 50 yards of felt for acoustic panels, and they said it had come in, so I stopped by there and picked it up.

I got home a little later and took the fabric downstairs. I looked around the porch, hoping my new software from Cakewalk has come. No luck. I headed downstairs a put on my "construction dude" hat.

The panels I'm making consist of a base of 1-inch thick pressed fiberglass covered on both sides with paper and foil covering. This is a fairly common type of wall insulation, but for my purposes, I have to remove the foil coving on the said

HERE I AM SLAVING AWAY OVER A HOT SCORE.

that faces out, exposing the fiberglass, which will tend to absorb rather than reflect sound. Then for further absorption (and aesthetics), the fabric is cut to wrap around the exposed part of the panel. It's attached with a spray adhesive, and stapled in the back.

All the panels have already been cut to form, and were waiting for the fabric. I spent the afternoon cutting and pasting. It's fairly slow-going though, since I have to allow the adhesive to dry overnight before putting the panel up on the wall.

I got several panels done, and made a Home Depot run for some electrical boxes in which the speaker connections will be mounted. I put the last two of those together, mounted them to the rear wall, and called it a day.

LESSONS/PROBLEMS

Well, this thing with Earthlink is beginning to be a real problem. They apparently still have me credit card number on file, even though I don't use them anymore. I think what is happening is that we set up another credit card to pay for the site, but when we got the big hit, that card rejected to bill, so it popped over to mine. Well, it's just something we'll have to slog through. All in all, though, I would rather be writing music!

Day 23 | **OCTOBER 7**

PREDICTIONS

- *Staff meeting.*
- *Probably more fooling around with Earthlink.*
- *Write some new library music.*

DIARY

Last night, when I got home, I found a FedEx door hanger that told me there was no one home when they tried to deliver, so I could pick up my package at FedEx after six. It was clearly my beloved "Foo" (Fujitsu computer), so I went and picked it up. It turned out that it was still under warranty, and they replaced the main board and the battery. Cool. Now I have my brain back, and didn't have to pay an arm and a leg.

This morning I went in, and we did the usual Tuesday morning staff meeting. It appears, I have a series of political spots to do next week, so I'll want to get the whole system shaken down by then. Everything seems to work, but this will be the first job I've done with the new computer. I also have to transfer some files that were on my Fujitsu that existed nowhere else for the last two weeks. It's a good thing they didn't have to reformat the disk.

Harmon handed me a copy of the contract with American Music Co. they had sent. It's pretty much a standard "work-for-hire" contract, meaning I work for them, and they own

THIS IS A SHOT OF THE ACTUAL FIRST BIG ORCHESTRA SCORE I EVER DID (IN 1984, OUCH!). IT WAS CALLED: "KENTUCKYSHOW" AND IT WAS INSTALLED IN A LARGE THEATRE IN LOUISVILLE. IT RAN FOR AROUND SEVEN YEARS.

everything I give them in exchange for xxx dollars. OK, I've seen and done this kind of thing before.

We met for a bit, and went through the contract, marking up anything we considered questionable, which were mostly the typos. After we get done with it, we'll send it back to AMC with our changes, and they can then change our changes and send it back. Such is the music business.

I went upstairs then to get my computer ready for its "maiden *voyage." It will be fine. Everything works, and I now have the old computer networked to it in case I need a backup. After I'm comfortable with the new system, I'll wipe most of the stuff off the old computer and use it as extra storage, but until then, I'm keeping it up as a redundant system.*

Having felt "inspired" by having a contract to sign, I decided to write some more music for AMC. The fact that they sent a contract means that the gig is on, so I may as well get as close as possible to finishing this new CD. It's about 98% there. I could just call it "done," but there's (almost) always room for one more.

The piece began with a militaristic feeling, so I ran with that. I have some very nice dramatic low strings that have a nice aggressive attack, so I started with those, bringing in some sharp, growling trombones for support, then introducing the main melody with a trumpet section. It began to feel good, with lots of action. This would make for some good background for a war movie (or a political ad).

After getting a minute or so into the piece (an hour or so of composition time per minute of music is a pretty reasonable rule of thumb for me, although it's not at all difficult to take sometimes much longer), I decided to take a break, and deal with some of this ongoing problem with Earthlink.

Jim Bloch and I talked about it. He had researched the thing, and found that, according to Earthlink, I was still the "owner" of the site, even though we had changed the credit card that

105

was to be billed. Apparently, the new credit card rejected the $26,000 they tried to charge it (imagine that!), and so they tried to charge it to the "owner." When that didn't work, they emailed me the bill.

The company had talked to them about the problem and agreed to pay a significantly reduced fee, since we didn't know that the video file our engineer had put up (for the benefit of the other employees) had gotten onto a list server, and suddenly the entire world was downloading it from our site. And Earthlink agreed because they failed to see any red flags go up when our hit count suddenly went from about a hundred hits a day to something like 15,000 (downloading video, no less!). So the amended bill came to a little over three grand, but instead of sending the company an invoice, they charged my card again, and this time the charge went through.

We decided the best thing to do would be for me to cancel out my Amex card totally, while we went through whatever we had to go through to change the "ownership" of the site. The company would then just reimburse me for the charges. I got on the horn with Amex, and did just that.

Afterwards, I went back to my "lab" to create more monsters. I almost got the militaristic piece finished, but around 5:00, there was still a bit of work left to do in the ending, by the end of the day, so I decided to get away from it (go home), and tackle it fresh in the morning.

LESSONS/PROBLEMS

In terms of problems, I'm just not going to go into the Earthlink thing! With regard to lessons, I think the entire affair demonstrates the power of the internet more than anything else I've seen. Being a small local media company, on average, we get maybe a couple hundred or so hits per day. Yet one video that arouses interest can make it onto some list servers, and suddenly the entire world is pinging your site. It's powerful, and could be a tremendous boon to advertising and marketing, AND dangerous, due to the fact that this sort of thing could happen to anyone with a website. Obviously ISPs like Earthlink do not mind one bit if your $19.95-per-month website suddenly runs up a bill in the tens of thousands. Caveat emptor!

THIS IS A SHOT OF THE KEYBOARD LAYOUT AT ELECTRONIC PHILHARMONIC WHEN I'M WORKING ON A LARGE PROJECT.

Day 24 | **OCTOBER 8**

PREDICTIONS

- Work on Sonar.
- Send off first CD proposal to AMC.
- Possible new music.

DIARY

Last night when I got home, I found another FedEx door tag. My software from Cakewalk ("Sonar") was in, so I swung by and picked it up.

This morning, I brought it in to the studio to install. I know there will be a bit of a learning curve to it, so I'm prepared to spend the entire day, and probably much of the next few days, working on it.

I stopped by the front desk and said "good morning" to Kim. She handed me a fax. It was the scripts from three political spots I'm to do next week, so I took them and Sonar and headed upstairs. I scanned the scripts quickly, and then went right to the computer.

The Sonar install went fine, and I did the online registration bit. Once it was installed, I started it up to have a look.

Even though Sonar is based on Cakewalk Pro Audio, this version is the third generation beyond it, and as one would expect from new software, with a new NAME as well, there were some substantial differences. The user interface was completely revamped. It has a very sleek look to it, but as I began to fool around with it, I began to notice that, while there were some very cool new things about it, there were other things that made me scratch my head.

Sonar is more closely integrated with digital audio now than it was before, so it's actually more similar to something like "Pro Tools" than to a normal a MIDI sequencer. It still retains MIDI capabilities, but it clearly is more audio-oriented.

This was evident as soon as I loaded an old Cakewalk MIDI file and played it. It was a simple one-track piano piece I use to test MIDI with, and it played it fine. So then I went to change the MIDI channel and play another instrument.

Hmmm. Where's the MIDI channel setting? Nothing on the track itself mentioned the channel. I clicked it, double-clicked it, right-clicked it, nothing! Of course, I have been used to the old Cakewalk that showed the MIDI channel, pan settings, volume settings, etc., right on the track, but none of that was there. Finally I noticed a little box in the corner of the screen that said: "Chn" and had a "one" in it. I highlighted it and typed in a "two." The sequence now played on channel 2. Seems a mighty strange way of assigning channels, but it's all part of the learning curve.

I went back to the track and started poking around on it. It seems you can maximize and minimize the track on the screen by clicking the usual buttons. When you maximize, you then see a little panel showing channel info, i/o info, program and bank settings, etc. It still seems more logical to me to put that stuff right on the line instead of making you go through two or three mouse clicks to find it, but there it was.

I went to the top menu. They still had the "insert" menu so I opened it up to insert a wave file, as I had before in Calkwalk Pro Audio (CPA). It had an item that said: "Insert Audio Track." I figured that must be it. Click!

Nope! That added a new, blank audio track to the project. OK, so where is the option for inserting an audio file? I poked around the "File" menu. Ah-ha! There it is! It's now called: "Import Audio." I loaded a music file into the track and played it. Then I started having some fun.

111

There are a number of new goodies included with Sonar, such as a Lexicon reverb plug-in, several new audio effects like compressors, limiters, graphic/parametric equalizers, a plug-in FX "rack," a "surround sound" processor, and a bunch of other toys. I started mangling the audio with effects.

This is the kind of thing you can spend the entire day doing, and that's just what I did. I played around with the audio toys for the rest of the afternoon, pausing only to look over some contracts we were about to send off to AMC. I signed the contract, put it together with a CD full of proposed new music, and handed it to Kim to send out.

Then I went back to my "padded room" and make funny noises for the rest of the afternoon.

LESSONS/PROBLEMS

Any new gear or software is going to present a laundry list of stuff you have to get used to, and Sonar is no exception. At the end of the day, it's a very capable program, and it will help me consolidate my music projects, so that an entire project can be done inside the computer, using virtual instruments, multi-track digital audio, and audio and MIDI processing. Then the entire project can be packed up into a single file and saved and backed up. It will undoubtedly simplify my life as time goes on, but I'll have to dig through some complexities to get there.

Day 25 | **OCTOBER 9**

PREDICTIONS

- *Work on Sonar.*
- *Work on Virtual Instruments.*
- *New strings.*

DIARY

Yesterday afternoon, my new Garritan string section collection arrived via FedEx. That gives me something musical to play with today. This is the first part of my new "orchestra" so I will want to get to work on it. I have ordered many sample/program collections in the past, but there is always a lot of tweaking I have to do to get third-party stuff to work the way I like it to.

Initially, I had planned on working some more with Sonar, particularly with the "virtual instruments" included with it, but I went right to the new strings. I began loading them up from the CD (there are six CDs, three in Akai format, three in Kurzweil format), and started playing with them. The set is divided into Violins, Violas, Cellos, and Bass, plus a combined string orchestra. I started playing with that first.

The sounds were lovely, very warm and rich, and most importantly, consistent all the way up and down. Each program uses instruments played loud (ff) and medium (mp) with key velocity switching between them. They include several basic expressions with each section, sustained notes with and without vibrato, marcato, spicato, martelle (three different note lengths), and one called "grand detache." This one is very good for most general purposes, because it is a fairly long (appx. two seconds) with a smooth attack and release. If I'm playing a part that keeps moving, it creates a very nice legato feeling, with a nice expressive rise and fall in intensity. I will want to combine this with a sustained string that I can instantly switch to if I need to hold a note or chord for longer than two seconds.

I spent quite a bit of time just loading and trying out sounds. Everything is very well recorded and consistent. There aren't as many expressions as I would have liked, there are no glissandi or slides between notes, grace notes, or very short stacatos, but on the whole, this is a big improvement over the very inconsistent strings I had been using.

I wrote a short piece to put the new stuff to the acid-test. It came out very nice, very believable. But I needed more control over sustains. So I began layering sample-sets together, first with the "grand detache" violins. I added a layer of sustained violins, but put them under mod-wheel control, so that with the wheel at zero, the sustains would not play at all, just the detaches. Then I made the wheel very sensitive, so that if it was up just a little, the sustains would join in, using the detache attack, but then holding the note. Because these strings are so consistently recorded, the sample switching is completely transparent and natural-sounding.

THIS IS THE AVID SYMPHONY AT WAVEWORKS, ANOTHER ALL-IN-ONE-BOX VIDEO WORKSTATION.

I then went on to apply the same programming to the violas, cellos, and basses. I now have a set of very realistic legato strings.

I wrote another short piece as a test, and was very happy with the result. Now I'm starting to get anxious to write some real music with this stuff, but there is still a fair amount of tweaking and programming to do.

The day was pretty much consumed by the strings, but as the afternoon wore on, I decided to give them a rest, and play around for a bit with the "virtual instruments" in Sonar. There is a "Virtual Sound Canvas," which is a model of the Roland general MIDI box, with the same sounds, most of which are not bad, but it's particularly difficult listening to the strings in that after the ones I've been working on. The Roland SC is useful for quick playback of general MIDI files, but not really for production.

Then I started playing with the "Vsampler," a virtual sample player that can load .WAV files into memory, or stream them from disk (there are several virtual instruments like this available now). I loaded a set of piano samples that came with it. They played back well, and sounded very nice, but it did not seem to be doing any velocity-switching of the softer and harder samples. There simply seemed to be a loud program, several medium programs, and a couple soft ones. Well, that wasn't very impressive, so I began to try to edit a program.

This is the point that separates the men from the boys when it comes to commercial programs. The capability is built into the software to do what you want, but many programmers write their software with the expectation that the end user is simply going to load and play programs. I am not one of those. I tend to get into the instrument and customize everything to my own tastes, and when I went into the editing pages of the Vsampler, I was greeted by an astonishing lack of a logical layout to the program. It was obvious in poking around that pretty much every parameter of every sample can be tweaked and massaged in a zillion different ways, but that was most of the problem.

There were so many parameters, it was virtually impossible to find the one that set up velocity-switching between sample sets. And every time I thought I found something that I thought should bring that up, such as clicking on a parameter called "velocity," I was taken to a new page with a graphic representation of the velocity curve for THAT PARTICULAR SAMPLE, which I could draw myself, mangle in a zillion ways, but NOT set up a velocity switch with any other sample!

Well, the frustration meter hit the red zone fairly quickly, and I bailed out of that one. Maybe I'll try it again another day, but this one was over.

LESSONS/PROBLEMS

Getting new software prepared for production use is always a matter of customization. There are guys in Hollywood who hire other guys as programmers to do this so that the composers can just say: "Give me a nice cello sound," and then play with it. Not so with me. I am in a far less exalted place in the industry, and my budget dictates that I do all that stuff myself. I upside of it is; I know what I want to have happen when I play, or hit a note hard, or move a mod wheel, and I set the system up to do just that. The downside is that I have to spend a lot of time programming that could be spent composing. But that's life in "Hollywood on the Potomac."

Day 26 | **OCTOBER 10**

PREDICTIONS

- More strings tweaking.
- More Sonar study.
- Prep for next week's spot series.

DIARY

Today is Friday, so I wanted to kind of get things put in place for a series of political ads I have to do next week. The client sent me scripts the other day, and I glanced at them, but was too busy playing with my new toys to look at it seriously. Now is the time to do just that, since the spots have to be produced by Wednesday.

Music for political advertising is a strange animal. It often has to be closely tailored to the candidate himself, lucky for me. Music that is strong and bold, juxtaposed with a candidate who is not exactly a very imposing presence can make him look silly. While warm and gentle, "homespun" sounding music would probably not sit well under a spot for Arnold Schwarzenegger, even if he's trying to put forward his "gentler" side. Yet there are also candidates who have a kind of weak voice and presence, who need strong musical support underneath.

This spot is for a guy running for a Senate seat. He's in his latter-forties, youthful-looking, good presence, and energy, so he probably won't need the music to "pump him up."

119

THIS IS MY INSTRUMENT RACK AND MIXER/HD RECORDER. ALL AUDIO GETS ROUTED FROM THE INSTRUMENTS THROUGH THE MIXER AND FINALLY INTO THE COMPUTER.

This is a series of three spots, each with a different focus. One is about the economy, another is about "jobs," and the third is the "home-and-family" spot. The client wants a running musical theme throughout, but each spot is to be treated on its own. That is why I wanted to work on a general thematic idea this week, and come back to the "nuts and bolts" next week. I started fooling around with a rhythmatic idea.

Most of the "baby-boom" generation came of age with rock and roll, and being that most political candidates of today come from that pool, the heavy rhythm section is not all that revolutionary an idea in this kind of advertising, although there are some general things to keep in mind (if you are planning to do this kind of work, make sure you have a good "French horn" sample).

The rhythm felt good, and I had a general melodic idea on the piano, so in the second half of the piece, I developed that a bit more with the orchestration. It is funny how the human mind thinks (or can be trained to think) in 15 to 30 second increments. In the first spot (the "economy" spot) the candidate was focusing on the dearth of jobs being created in the current "recovery," and, of course, how he would correct this situation. The second half was to focus on what the candidate intended to do about it. So I divided the spot roughly into those two halves, with a feeling of a bit more "concern" in the front half, and a greater hopefulness and optimism in the second.

I came up with what I felt would make a decent demo of the general idea, saved my work, and headed home.

LESSONS/PROBLEMS

I didn't have a lot of problems to speak of today, but there is something of a lesson here. There is always a two-year gap between election years (four years between the "big" ones), and a couple years can change the direction of the aesthetic winds considerably. Many of my clients want to reach out to *the more likely voters, meaning those past forty or so. But still, they don't want to ignore that huge demographic that buys into body-piercing and tattoos.*

"Rock And Roll" may have been revolutionary as a musical form when the boomers were young, but now, it's just plain old rock and roll, and there isn't that generational brick wall in popular music anymore. Advertisers are even using old Led Zeppelin songs to sell Cadillacs! The composer of today has a much greater amount of freedom to play with modern musical ideas than did his predecessors back in the days of long hair and army fatigues.

Hey Hey, Hi Hi, Rock and Roll will Never Die! Just make sure you don't forget that French horn.

Day 27 | **OCTOBER 13**

PREDICTIONS

- *Music for three political ads.*
- *Get with Harmon and Brenda about this Earthlink thing.*

DIARY

Got into work around the usual time. I have real client work to do today, so I get to kind of shake down my new system and see how it works on a real project.

I talked to Paul first thing, and he said he got a couple of off-line edits (MPEGS) of the spots from the client by email. So I asked him to put them up on the server someplace and I can get them. He did and I did.

The first new way of doing stuff is to use lock video to the music right in the computer, rather than to have Paul lay off a copy on three-quarter-inch video. I have done music to computer video before in Cakewalk Pro Audio, but the sync was not very tight. I loaded the MPEG into Sonar, and started playing in some MIDI tracks along with it. The sync was nice and tight and reliable. Good. Now maybe I can finally get rid of this wheezy old three-quarter.

I imported the MIDI file with the music I did Friday into Sonar and put it against the picture. With a couple of nips and tucks, I got it lined up nicely with the video, and trimmed it down to 60 seconds.

That was easy enough. Unfortunately the client wasn't going to be here until around noon, so I had to wait to get approval of the musical direction.

When he got in, though, the first thing he did was come to see me and I played the piece with the video for him. He liked the music, but told me the end was changing and a graphic overlay would come up at a certain spot, and he wanted kind of a crescendo there. I said that wouldn't be a problem, and as soon as Paul had the new edit with the graphic done, he could just send me a new MPEG.

The client also told me they hadn't made up their minds whether the third spot was to have music or not. That's not a problem either way, really. I'm here all day.

Paul sent me the updated video and a ruff of the second spot after about an hour, and I tweaked in a nice, lush crescendo with the graphic and played it for the client. He was good to go with it. Too bad not every day is this easy. I set to work on the next spot.

This was generally like the first spot, but in this case, the candidate was talking about the flat job growth in his state, and the client wanted to open with a little more "concern" in the music. The positive theme came in a few seconds later, so I timed the existing music from a visual change right after the candidate's first statement. Then I put a low sting chord under the first line. It seemed to work OK, so I played it for the client.

THIS IS THE "OFFICIAL" SHOT OF ME FOR WAVEWORKS PROMO AND STUFF.

Again, he liked it, and by the way, they decided to use music in the third spot after all, but I wouldn't get that video until tomorrow. That's not a big problem since they already signed off on the first two spots.

Since I had some time on my hands, I talked to Harmon about the Earthlink thing, since my American Express already paid $3100 to Earthlink. The company is simply going to reimburse me for the charge. That's the simplest way of doing it, so that's fine. I then called Amex and cancelled my existing

THIS IS MY MAIN COMPUTER AT WAVEWORKS. IT'S A 3 GHZ MACHINE WITH A 160 GB HARD DRIVE. I HAVE SINCE MOVED IT AND THE OTHER EQUIPMENT TO MY HOME STUDIO, AND AM FINDING THAT IT'S GETTING EASIER TO FILL UP EVEN THAT MUCH DISK SPACE.

account, and started up a new one. That should settle this thing (although I have learned through experience that reality has a habit not always agreeing with our expectations).

I finished out the day playing with the new string samples. I didn't use them in the current set of spots, because the orchestration of them is more sparse, and they weren't completely set up to my liking yet. Still, they are quite good, and I'm looking forward to using them on a new project.

LESSONS/PROBLEMS

This was not a particularly problematic day. My client is one I have worked with for a number of years, so I know their habits and tastes fairly well, and they know what they can expect from me. Having a long-standing relationship with a client allows for a greater amount of creative freedom, usually because over the years, you gain a handle on the specifics of their demands, and at what point they might consider your ideas "overboard." Also there is a lot less hand-holding that has to go on, because the client knows the process, and is comfortable that they are not going to be unpleasantly surprised.

THIS IS WHERE I KEEP MY SAMPLE LIBRARY CDS. THIS AMOUNTS TO ROUGHLY 90 HOURS OF INSTRUMENT SOUNDS AND EFFECTS.

Day 28 | **OCTOBER 14**

PREDICTIONS

- Staff meeting.
- Finish third political ad.
- Paperwork, backups.

DIARY

This is staff meeting morning, so we did that first thing. We went over what was happening this week, including the spots I'm working on. As I finish the music for these things, I hand that off the Ian, who marries the music to the video and does the final mix. The first two are done, so now he's waiting for me to finish the last one, which I have to start on this morning.

Paul put an MPEG of the spot on the server for me, and I grabbed it and had a look. This is the "home and family" spot, with the candidate, his wife, their 1.57 children, and of course, their dog. (I have noticed over the years that I have never done a political ad in which the candidate is shown with the family cat.)

Anyway, this means I have to do a "warm and fuzzy" version of the theme. The first two I did were more energetic, but this one has to be quite a bit more laid-back. I decided to center it around piano. First I played a slower and prettier version of the main theme on piano and played it against the spot. In this one, there were no important changes or "hit points" that I had to accent musically. This one was just background.

After I was satisfied with the piano part, I added some strings. I have a very nice string section that is a very large orchestra in a large hall, and it has a very warm, although not very distinct, kind of sound, so it's good for playing nice warm chords behind other instruments, but not very good for moving lines.

I worked nicely, and as the finishing touch, I gave it that

WHERE THIS GUY CAME FROM, I DO NOT KNOW!

"never-fails" element that political ads cannot seem to do without, a French horn, playing the concluding melody line over the strings. The one thing I had to make sure of was that the music concluded a little early, and rung out for about a second so that the narrator could get in the obligatory "paid for by blah blah blah for Congress."

That finished, I played it for the client, and again, they were happy with it. Life is good!

I did a final mix and put it up on the server for Ian to grab. We have been moving stuff like that around the shop now for a while, and it works very well. Everything we do is in some kind of computer, and each one can accept a number of different file formats for their media. Ian is using a Pro Tools system that can take AIFFs or WAV files, as well as several others, so I sent him a WAV being that that's the native format of my computer.

It was time to close out the project and back everything up. I did my backup routine and filled out the paperwork to go to Kim, who then tracks all the time and expenses for billing.

With all that stuff done, and half the day still left, I decided to play around with Sonar a bit more. For this project, I didn't get into it very much as an audio system, mostly since I wasn't used to it. I just used it to sync my MIDI tracks with the video, and it worked fine. But now, I wanted to play around with some of the audio features in it, and there are quite a few.

I loaded a piece for the AMC library project that I had done a week or so ago, and started playing with some of the audio effects that are available. I pulled up a multi-band compressor plug-in and started playing with it.

This is an orchestral piece, so compression is usually not the first tool you reach for when playing with the sound. Compression of all sorts works better on rock and pop music for when you want to get the sound up "in your face," by reducing the dynamics of the piece. Orchestra music depends

HERE ARE SOME OF THE MORE "ESOTERIC" INSTRUMENTS I HAVE USED IN VARIOUS PROJECTS. CLOCKWISE FROM 11:00, A AUSTRAIAN "EMU CHASER", A "STARBRIGHT", MY PAIR OF MUSICAL BALLS, AN ALTO RECORDER, AND, YES, WELCOME TO HELL! THAT IS AN ACCORDION!

on wide dynamics, so compression should be used sparingly. However, since I was just playing, I decided to do some radical stuff.

I set the multiband for a hard-knee setting and played the piece. Yep, sure enough, it made the entire piece very loud, but killed the dynamics. So I fooled around with softer settings, and eventually I found one that worked fairly nicely, although it was subtle. I saved a copy of the piece with the compression

THIS IS THE KEYBOARD SETUP AT WAVEWORKS. ON TOP IS AN ANCIENT ENSONIQ SQ-80 THAT I USE AS A MASTER KEYBOARD. IT HAS A SURPRISINGLY GOOD BASIC SEQUENCER BUILT IN THAT I STILL USE OFTEN FOR QUICK SKETCHES AND WORKING OUT BASIC PARTS. IT HAS AN "ORGAN-LIKE", MEANING NON-WEIGHTED, KEYBOARD ACTION.

just so I could "A-B" the two sometime when my ears were fresher.

Next I pulled up an EQ. There are several EQs available, the one I started playing with was a combination graphic/parametric EQ with six sweepable bands and a graphic plotter. Very nice. It's easy to just make quick changes using the virtual "sliders," but you can also grab a frequency band with the mouse, and move it up or down for level, or left and right to sweep through frequency ranges. This is very cool *if you feel that somewhere, there is just some gap in the frequency range and you want to find it.*

I spent the rest of the afternoon experimenting with EQs, effects, compressors, limiters, etc., but didn't use it on any real music yet. I don't recommend this sort of thing if you are on a deadline, and have to maintain your objectivity about the sound. The more you play with this stuff, the more your ear loses touch with reality.

But it is necessary to find out what everything does (or doesn't do), so this kind of thing is part of the experience of learning new software, and a very fun part, because you can pretty radically mangle sound with this new generation of computer-based signal processors. In doing so, every so often you find a new trick that makes you think "Oh wow, I know what I can use THIS for"!

LESSONS/PROBLEMS

Once again, a relatively problem-free day. It's always good to work with long-time clients whose needs and tastes you know very well. But it can't always be like that, so it's important to keep an open mind. And a long-time client can often surprise you by wanting something unusual from you. It's what keeps this business interesting.

Day 29 | **OCTOBER 15**

PREDICTIONS

- Work on new library piece.
- Put Sonar to real-world test.

DIARY

I checked my email first thing this morning and got a note from my guy at AMC. He was happy with most of what I sent him, but there were a couple pieces he felt would be more appropriate to CDs based on other styles, so I need to come up with a few new things for the "heroic/adventure" CD.

This gives me a chance to put Sonar through the real-world acid test. I have had some fun playing around with the effects and plug-ins so far, but now I want to see how far I can stretch it before something gives. I began by coming up with a little horn-based melody, sort of reminiscent of an "Indiana Jones" kind of score.

With that, I started to orchestrate. Instead of using Sonar at first, I used my trusty old Cakewalk, which is much less capable, but much faster and easier to work with when doing purely MIDI-based stuff. I'm also armed with new strings and the other orchestral stuff I have been putting together for this thing, so I loaded up some orchestral brass, strings, and percussion, and started to work.

This is a very "active" piece, that is to say there is a lot of musical movement going on in it. The horns doing the main melody line sail over the top, and under them is a bunch of strings moving around furiously. The new strings have a very nice, clean attack to them, so this kind of stuff is a lot easier than before.

I am also being very conscious of the placement of instruments in the stereo field. I want this to have as good a "space" as I can make it, so I'm splitting instruments up in ways that maximize this. The horns doing the main melody are panned center/right slightly, with a trumpet section that plays an answer line in the beginning coming more from the left. The strings are spread out in a more normal orchestral seating arrangement.

Once I got the main body of the first part of the piece done, I then removed all the effects from all the instruments, and laid them of to audio tracks on my DPS-16. Then I imported them as WAV files into Sonar.

Among the effects Sonar includes is an excellent Lexicon reverb plug-in that allows you to manipulate the size of the room, early reflections, high-frequency damping, etc. It also allows you as many instances of the plug-in as you wish, so instead of creating a single effects bus and routing the tracks to it, I put a separate instance of the Lexicon onto each track, and played with the parameters according to the way they might react in a real hall. The brass would be farther back in the *field, for example, so they would have a little faster early reflection and a bit deeper reverberation than the strings in front of them. Also, since the string lines are so busy, I don't want them to get "soupy" in the reverb.*

So far, so good. I'm starting to get some very nice "space" in this thing, thanks to the new reverbs, which are much cleaner and more "airy" than the old stuff I was using. The first part of the piece, where I introduce the main theme, is done. Now for the fun.

I want to create a little romantic interlude to give some contrast to the piece. This will be done mostly with strings. Again, I went back to the old Cakewalk to get the basic tracks done for this. Because it's going to go straight to digital audio after I compose it, I'm going to set up an orchestration in the Kurzweil more optimized to the strings. I pulled out my best stuff, and again being careful to place the instruments consistently with the first part, started writing.

Once the interlude was done, I recorded that into the multi-track and transferred it to Sonar, appending it to the end of the main theme. In Sonar, there is no fixed number of audio or MIDI tracks, so I put the strings on completely new, blank tracks. Again, I plugged the Lexicon reverb into the tracks and played with the settings until I was getting some good dimension in the sound. I also added a couple MIDI tracks to play a few additional parts along with the audio tracks.

Hey, I think I like working this way. All the tracks sync together

THIS IS A SHOT OF THE MUSIC ROOM AT WAVEWORKS IN MCLEAN. EVERYTHING IS SET UP IN AN "L" FOR EASY ACCESS, AND THE MAIN RACK IS IN THE MIDDLE.

wonderfully, the outboard MIDI gear does as well, and if I need to put some single audio sample, such as a cymbal crash or something, into the piece, I can just load it from the disk and place it wherever I want it. There are a lot more options available now than there were before. I know I need to beware of getting caught in "the Hell of too many options," but right now, I'm having fun.

LESSONS/PROBLEMS

Everything is working very smoothly, which always scares me a bit, but I'm getting some real work done, and in pretty good time, even considering the learning curve. The one thing I need to be careful of, though, is that because I have so many different options available to me now, it will be easy to create a product that is a mish-mosh of them that might be unwieldy, and could cause problems if I have to go back and rework something. I also need to come up with a new backup methodology.

THIS IS THE INSTRUMENT RACK THAT'S CONTROLLED BY THE COMPUTER. AT THE TOP IS A FOSTEX DS RDAT THAT I USE FOR MASTERING. BELOW THAT IS A KURZWEIL K2500 THAT IS THE MAIN WORKHORSE OF THE SYSTEM. BELOW THAT IS A KURZWEIL MICRO-PIANO MODULE AND A CD-ROM DRIVE THAT FEEDS THE K2500.

Day 30 | **OCTOBER 16**

PREDICTIONS

- Finish the new library piece.
- New score coming from Harmon.
- Figure out how to backup everything.

DIARY

I got in the usual time this morning and (after getting coffee, of course) went straight to work on the new library piece. I

THIS IS AN AVID DS NITRIS, A HI-DEF CAPABLE EDITING BOX. OFTEN TIMES THE VIDEO IS FINISHED IN HERE, COMPLETE WITH MUSIC, AUDIO, SWEETENING, GRAPHICS, AND THE WHOLE SHEBANG.

wanted to get that finished before Harmon gives me something else to do. First, though, I checked my email.

I got a note from the people I bought the new Kuzweil from. Oh no! They're not going to ship it until next week! This is why I hate "preordering" anything. The stuff invariably gets held up for some reason, and I'm left chewing the woodwork!

I heaved a heavy sigh, and loaded up what I needed to drown my sorrows in work.

I finished the "romantic interlude" yesterday, so today I wanted to come up with a nice dramatic restatement of the main theme. "restatement" is one of those things computers do very well, but of course, they don't just "restate," they duplicate. While it can be real handy to have an exact duplicate of a part you want to repeat, in most music, and in orchestral music particularly, the repetition shouldn't be exact, but have a bit more pizzazz, some slight changes to the parts that give it force, especially toward the conclusion.

I took my duplicate of the beginning and moved several parts around, doubling the strings with a flute in one case, adding a low French horn in another. Then, after the first (re)statement of the main melody, I repeated it in a new key with added trumpets and a countermelody on the French horns and trombones. Now it builds into something a little more unexpected before going back into the main theme.

That theme then plays though as before, but again with a few of the parts altered and additional octave of strings doubled here, a horn and harp embellishment there, and so on. Then I brought the whole piece to a nice big close, with all the instruments play a tutti.

Now it was time to mix. The new MIDI parts were added on top of the existing audio in Sonar, so they had to be recorded into audio tracks now. I sync'ed up the DPS-16 and the computer, and laid off the parts (there were seven new tracks). Then I imported them into Sonar from the shared hard drive,

145

THIS WAS MY HOME STUDIO SETUP WHILE I WAS AT WAVEWORKS. THE MAIN KEYBOARD IS A KURZWEIL 2661, WHICH IS COMPATIBLE WITH MY K2500 AT WORK, SO I CAN SIMPLY HAUL FILES BACK AND FORTH ON DISK, OR RETRIEVE THEM FROM THE NET FROM OUR SERVER WHEN I'M HOME.

placing them at the end of their respective tracks, violins in the violin track, and cellos in the cello track, etc.

The nice thing about doing things this way is that all the same audio settings, reverbs, EQs, and so on, are consistent with the newly added parts. There are no audible differences that would make the listener sense that there had been an edit in the audio (even though there was).

Once that was done, I set up to write the automation into the

THIS IS MY "BRAIN". IT'S A FUJITSU 4110. I USE IT FOR ALMOST EVERYTHING BUSINESS-WISE, BUT IT ALSO DOUBLES AS A REMOTE CONTROLLER FOR MY OTHER COMPUTERS.

back end of the mix, making sure that I don't get too carried away by the climax that I "bury the needles." After about a half-hour of mix time, I was satisfied. The piece sounds and feels good, the orchestra has very nice dimension to the sound, thanks in part to these nice new reverb plug-ins, and a listener would be hard-pressed to tell it isn't a real orchestra.

The goal is to eventually make it impossible to tell the difference. I don't know if that really can be done, but we're getting closer all the time.

LESSONS/PROBLEMS

Well, I ended up using the whole day on the new library piece, but that was OK because Harmon didn't have any video for me to look at anyway. And it gave me a chance to really put this new stuff to a real-world test before I started using for client projects. I feel pretty confident of all this stuff now, and even though I haven't really gotten half-way into the capabilities, I know my way around enough to get real work done efficiently, and without any nasty surprises. Of course, those words may get eaten tomorrow!

WHAT I'M DOING NOW

Two years have passed since I wrote my career diary. Much of what I wrote about was related to the gradual transformation of the music-creation process via the constant, and not-so-gradual transformation of technology.

Well, much has changed since then. The new music system I was writing about has been moved to the studio in my house, upgraded, expanded and tweaked, and I have formed my own production company. I have been working with some local clients I worked with in the past, but also with new clients from New York, California, Canada, the UK, Europe, Australia, and all over the globe, as if they were right down the street, thanks to the internet.

My new company is called: Electronic Philharmonic (sounds a bit on the high-falooting side of the spectrum I suppose, but marketing is marketing after all) and we specialize in orchestral music for film, TV and media, produced primarily using technology.

The CD project I was working on at the time has been finished and released, and the music is available from American Music Company (www.americanmusicco.com). I am currently in production of another CD for the same folks, with a contract for a third after that.

I did in fact add the East-West/Quantum Leap Symphonic Orchestra library to my sample collection, and I use it extensively.

Demos of my recent work, including several compositions that were mentioned in the diary, are available for a listen at www.electronic-philharmonic.com.

Well, enough of that. On to the stuff that makes an epilogue an epilogue; reflections on the things I wrote about, as seen through the prism of the passage of time.

Well, first of all, technology marches on. One of the most intriguing examples of how that works is the fact (I recently realized) that I have not delivered a client project to the client on any kind of physical media for over a year. All the demos I have sent to clients in the past 12+ months have been MP3 files delivered via email, and all final masters were either directly placed into video through a server at the video facility, or delivered via FTP. I have only used CDs and DVDs as project backups or as mail-out demos.

In the past year, the amount of music I sell per month from my library via the internet has multiplied 15 times! I have been told by some of the clients for whom I compose that their ratio of internet sales vs. physical media is up by about the same amount.

I have been able to walk into studios and facilities with masters on my laptop hard drive, and then send them to a server via a wireless connection.

For Christmas, I got my wife an XM satellite radio, and now the music we play around the house all day comes from outer space.

We are clearly moving rapidly toward a world in which music is no longer delivered on something round with a hole in the middle. What this means remains to be seen. Perhaps the time will come when one can simply buy a lifetime subscription to a music label's entire catalog, and just pull any cut from it out of the air to some iPod-like device anytime they wish. Perhaps it will be considered a "public utility," like water or sewage service.

For composers like me, these technological/societal changes represent a real challenge. On the one hand, there is the opportunity to get more music out to more people the world over, faster than ever before. But there is also the downside; that this whole "better, faster, cheaper" paradigm demands that I continually produce my music better and faster, and sell it much cheaper, since now my competition isn't confined to a few other guys in my metropolitan area, but it's every other composer on the planet.

One hopes that all this advancement in communications technology will ultimately serve to promote a kind of "meritocracy" within the musical arts/business. But dumb luck is also a factor, and that cannot be replicated in software.

I got into this business by running into a few guys at parties. I suppose I could do the same sort of thing within the "blogosphere," but it doesn't sound like as much fun.

And of all the things I have learned over my career, one of the most important is that "fun" is not an option. "Fun" is absolutely vital.